FINDING BALANCE

101 concepts for taking better care of self

DAN ROSIN, PH.D.

Copyright © 2023 Dan Rosin, Ph.D.

All rights reserved. No part of this book may be reproduced, stored, or transmitted by any means—whether auditory, graphic, mechanical, or electronic—without written permission of both publisher and author, except in the case of brief excerpts used in critical articles and reviews. Unauthorized reproduction of any part of this work is illegal and is punishable by law.

ISBN: 979-8-88640-523-1 (sc)
ISBN: 979-8-88640-524-8 (hc)
ISBN: 979-8-88640-525-5 (e)

Because of the dynamic nature of the Internet, any web addresses or links contained in this book may have changed since publication and may no longer be valid. The views expressed in this work are solely those of the author and do not necessarily reflect the views of the publisher, and the publisher hereby disclaims any responsibility for them.

One Galleria Blvd., Suite 1900, Metairie, LA 70001
1-888-421-2397

DEDICATION

I dedicate this book to the many caregivers I have had the privilege of serving during my 40-year journey in the helping professions.

Everybody dies, but not everyone lives.
(William Wallace)

CONTENTS

Acknowledgements ix
Preface xi

I Can Have Fun on a School Night! 1
Balance 4
P + P = P 5
Teeter-Totter 7
Today a Choice, Tomorrow a Lifestyle 8
Conscious vs. Automatic 9
Starting Over 10
Permission to Try New Things 11
Better 13
Change 14
Understandable but No Longer Appropriate 15
Systems Don't Like to Change 16
If It Isn't Working, Change It! 17
Good Stuff Journal 18
Energy 19
To Feel Good Requires Energy 20
Quiet Energy 21
Life Force vs. Lifestyle Energy 22
It's Never Too Late to Have a Happy Childhood 23
Project vs. Time Thinking 25
Work vs. Real Life 26
A, B, or C Pile – You Choose! 28
Kiss the Bricks Goodbye (thanks, Donald Meichenbaum) 30
The Key Hour for Evening Energy 31
Work vs. Health Messages 32

Ego vs. Health	34
Slurp It Up	36
Stew Juice	38
Don't Stew – Do!	39
Play Isn't Nice – It's Imperative	40
Planned Spontaneity	41
Spice is a Necessity for a Balanced Lifestyle	42
Negative Thoughts can be Controlled	43
Woody Allen	44
No Me! No Us! Only the Project!	45
What Happened to the "We" in Our Relationship?	46
Active Listening	47
Love and Needs	49
Courtesy vs. Permission	50
Wellness Continuum	51
Relationships and the Wellness Continuum	52
Be Married to Your Principles, but Not the Outcomes	53
Applying the "Be Married" Concept to Depression	55
The "I," "You," and "We" Language Possibilities	57
Panic Attack – For What Purpose?	58
Decide or Others Will	59
Watch Your Language	60
What Do I Want?	61
Who Am I?	62
Drama Triangle	63
Responsible vs. Helpful	65
Stop Collecting Other People's Monkeys	67
"Nice" and "Pleasing" Just Don't Work	68
To Be an 8…Congruency and Self-Love are the Key, Not a Relationship	70
Third Family	72
Backyard	73
Number One (#1)	75
Duplication	76
Gap	77

Could Have Been	78
You Can't Fix It Where It Got Broken	79
Buffer Time	80
Worry vs. Concern	81
Speed Bump	82
I Used To…	83
Universal Truth – Yours or Mine?	84
You're Not It…	86
Powerlessness Á Frustration Á Anger	88
Anger Begets Anger	89
Strokes and Conscientious Objectors	90
Pleasing and Placating – Early "How To Make It" Messages	92
Healthy vs. Unhealthy Strokes	94
Change the Filter from Accomplishment to Health	95
Diversify	96
The Law of Diminishing Returns	97
Crummy Strokes	100
Dependent on Others?	101
80–20 Rule	102
Too High a Price	103
Jealousy is About Lack of Self-Esteem	104
Why Now?	105
After the Burnout…	107
Workplace Trauma and a Commitment to Health	108
Pushing and Punishing (Pu + Pu)	109
The Half Empty Syndrome	111
Declaring vs. Fear of Failure	114
Lifestyle is the Goal…Health is the Means	115
Purpose	116
Lower the Bar and Raise Your Spirits	117
Move Your Feet	118
Deflection Theory	119
Killer Words	120

My Roots: Education
- Take Care of Self First 121
- Stand and Deliver 123
- Professional 125
- Educators Ought to Buy Season Tickets to Everything 126
- If You Can't Stand the Heat, Get Out of the Kitchen 128
- Badminton on the Ed Sullivan Show (Just Like Teaching) 130
- Discipline and the Three Cs 132
- Dispenser of Positive Reminders 133
- Nobody Gets in My Way of Teaching 134

Philosophical Dilemma 136

Appendix A Six Dimensions of Wellness 138
Appendix B Balanced Educator Award (BEA) 140
Appendix C Glossary 141

ACKNOWLEDGEMENTS

Thanks to my many clients who, over the years, have taught me much more than I taught them.

Thank you to my family—Drinda, whose love keeps me grounded; Lisa, who taught me the difference between parenting theory and reality; and Brad, who lives out my beliefs about wellness.

Thank you to Don S. Williams for taking the time to understand what I wrote and then improving the communication of those ideas.

Thank you to Gloria Zasitko for your patience and many rewrites. Thank you to Cory Clark and Brian Hydesmith for your creativity and support.

Thank you to Jenny Gates and Stu Slayen for your gifts and guidance in editing this hodge-podge.

Thank you to my mother, Emerald, for her love and belief that I could do anything I chose to do. I spent the last days of her life beside her, working on this book.

And thank you, the reader, whose thirst for information, knowledge, and a better life have led you to this book.

PREFACE

For more than four decades, I have worked with clients, students, parents, caregivers, and others to help solve their living issues. My therapeutic time with them has often been reduced by an on-target teaching concept, such as those that fill the pages of this book. These concepts help to cut to the chase and invite understanding and insight with the least amount of verbiage. The concepts are the result of the interaction between clients and myself (1+1 = more than 2), and I share them with the hope that readers will find value in their message and will take better care of themselves.

Read on and **learn**.

Use and **improve**.

I CAN HAVE FUN ON A SCHOOL NIGHT!

A very important lesson resulted from an extremely tense moment in my life.

As is the case for most educators/counsellors, I have too much to do and too little time in which to do it. When I checked my schedule one fateful morning, I realized I had agreed to give a one-hour presentation on wellness at 1:00 p.m. that day to a dozen or so people. I was not prepared but did not consider one hour of wellness to 15 people a problem, since I had done it many times before.

I set off for my destination in Brandon, Manitoba, a 130-mile trip, with barely two hours to get there. I did not know the name of the conference I was addressing and certainly had not organized any notes. However, I felt reasonably confident that I wouldn't need any notes for this one-hour presentation. I would just interact with the participants.

At exactly 1:00 p.m., I arrived at the Victoria Inn and went inside in search of Ballroom A. When I found the room, I discovered it was packed with approximately 300 people. "Whoops, wrong room!" Then I did the only thing a visual-type person could do under the circumstances and went looking for another Ballroom A. That picture of 300 people did not match the one of 15 still in my head. Of course, I was being ridiculous, and sheepishly returned to the original room and peeked in. A person appeared, dramatically relieved, started breathing again, and rushed up to me.

The professional development chairperson for the conference gave me a big crushing hug, which made me feel instantly welcome, and suddenly suspicious. She started to lead me to the front of the room, but my firm grip on the doorframe prevented her from taking me anywhere. She suddenly realized something was not right. "Oh, did they not inform you about the change?" "What…ah…change?" I stammered. My apprehension was driving the panic. "You are now the conference's closing speaker and speaking for two hours—and we're late!" I was suddenly totally alone, totally brain dead, and drenched in my own perspiration.

As I shuffled toward the gallows, ah, podium, my mind was racing. *I don't have a single note on which to base my address. I have two hours to sum up and evaluate a conference I have not attended. In fact, I don't even know the name of the conference, nor its theme. On top of all that, I'm brain dead. If I'm asked for the names of my children, I will have to ask for clues!*

The introduction was finally finished—all too soon, I needed more time to think—by this person I had never met before, and she turned to me and said "…I am proud to introduce Dr. Dan Rosin to you all." The word "all" seemed to echo through a vast reverberation chamber. "Proud" seemed doomed for replacement.

Have you ever made the laborious trip down to the basement to fetch something, only to find that when you get there, you haven't the faintest notion what you wanted? That your mind was a blank? Well, that was me, nothing in my mind, a total blank!

Out of this absolute void of uninspired non-thoughts came a faint voice—my mother's. She cried out a message that would save me from that pit of despair and embarrassment into which I was sinking deeper and deeper each minute. My mother said, *you are not supposed to have fun on a school night. Save your best time and energy for school.* For sure, I had lost it!

Imagine! I was 54 years old, my mother was "speaking" to me as I stood in front of 300 eagerly waiting, anticipatory people, and she is saying that I'm not supposed to have fun on a school night. Five out of seven nights I am not supposed to have fun! And that's all my facsimile of a brain could dredge up from my vast storehouse of knowledge.

I did the unthinkable. I went with it. I said it out loud. I didn't know what the audience was thinking, but they seemed to be approving. Hopefully, they thought that I was beginning my meticulously prepared presentation: *Oh good. Very clever. He jumps right into the theme. A good beginning.* I continued.

"How many of you subscribe to a similar message that says you are not supposed to have fun on a school night?" I wasn't entirely sure what that really meant, but it sounded pretty good. I held my breath; I believed I could hear the audience's thoughts, but perhaps it wassimply wishful thinking: *He asks us a question to get focused. Great technique. This guy knows what he is doing.* To be honest, I dared hope for only a few responses—even one. So, when the majority put up their hands, I started breathing again. And for the next two hours we explored the message, "I am not supposed to have fun on a school night," its origin, and the debilitating effect that it's had on our lives to date.

I'm sure I am not overstating the impact of this message as "debilitating" when you think that five out of seven nights you are not supposed to have fun, but rather save that energy for something more important, such as your work. Five out of seven nights are work nights, and out of the other two, if you're not too tired, one might be used for play. By the end of the work week, many of us are exhausted and just want to hit the sofa and be left alone.

In addition to the "no fun on a school night" belief, many of us subscribe to the notion that if we are not working all the time, as we have been programmed to do, then the only other available options if we want or need downtime are sickness or fatigue. If we want time away from work, we make ourselves so sick or so fatigued that we can then take some guilt-free time off for ourselves. Pitiful!

We need to learn to have fun every day, and not save it up for the two days on the weekend, or a couple of weeks of summer holidays. Let's learn how to have fun and seek balance, every day.

If we are to get and stay healthy, we best challenge my mother's message and change the belief to:

I <u>can</u> have fun on a school/work night!

BALANCE

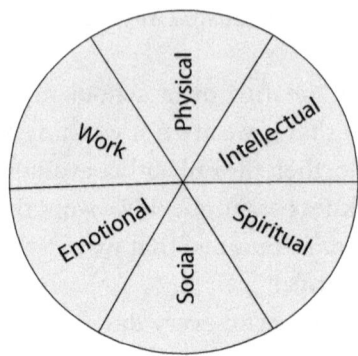

In working with a great many people who exhibit symptoms of burnout and depression, have nothing more to give, and just want to be left alone, I have come to understand their symptoms as an issue of imbalance. Being "in balance" is the key to physical and psychological health. People must understand and actively practice a balanced lifestyle as exemplified by the Six Dimensions of Wellness— Emotional, Intellectual, Work, Spiritual, Physical, and Social (see Appendix A).

Much could be said about the importance of balance in our lives. Good lifestyle choices based on sound holistic principles give you a significantly better chance at feeling better—physically and psychologically.

> *Focusing on health is much like investing*
> *in a retirement account. Contribute a little each*
> *day and it will pay huge dividends in the future.*

P + P = P

Often when I talk about the necessity of balance in a person's life, I refer to the concepts of **Patience, Pace,** and **Protection**.

People are getting sick at an alarming rate because they are out of balance. They need to make changes so they can get healthy. They need to figure out how to "have a life" and do their job, to establish **time** and **energy boundaries**. Hopefully, it will not be too late, and will be before they get sick. This decision to take care of self is integrally woven with self-esteem, self-worth, and permission to be in **balance** and to set **boundaries**.

The reality is that you can establish or commit to being in balance and set both energy and time boundaries, and you will be different! However, the people around you will still be the same, expecting you to continue being *nice*, *extremely helpful*, and the *no-waves-at-all-costs* person you have always been.

Patience is about dealing with other people's expectations for you. People in your life (friends, colleagues, clients, family, neighbors) will continue to want a piece of your time and energy. Just because they expect that from you is not a reason for you to continue meeting their expectations or to get frustrated and angry with them, and end up harming yourself. When you get angry, there is internal cell damage and it takes seconds off your life each time.

Rather than undisciplined anger, the healthier way to deal with their expectations is with patience. Thank them for thinking of you, for wanting you, for valuing you. However, having thought it out, your final response might be something like, "Despite what you want from me, this is what I'm prepared to do."

They won't necessarily like your decision and will attempt to change your mind, usually through guilt and intimidation. So be persistent. You will have to really believe you're worthwhile, and that you are entitled to a life. It won't be easy, but people are trainable.

Pacing, as I mean and apply the word, is to change the speed at which you live, to stay at a lower gear especially when others around you are getting hyper. We accelerate and hardly even notice the speed at which we lead our daily lives. Is this sped-up life part of the stress syndrome that is referred to in the literature? You bet!

To help people realize they are sped up, and then to get them to purposely slow down for health reasons, I use the **hypnotic voice** technique with my clients. I learned about my hypnotic voice from my intuitive daughter, Lisa, who, when she was a teenager, would accuse me of using my counselling voice. This later became my hypnotic voice, particularly when she got upset and we were attempting to have a discussion. Apparently, when having a vigorous discussion or an all-out argument with a teenager, you are not supposed to lower your voice, talk slower, ask more questions than give answers, or plant positive ideas, because it becomes "…very hard to argue with you, and that's not fair."

Although this insight—hypnotic voice—was learned as a result of contact with my teenagers (I also have a son) it applies equally to adults. The prime reason for using your hypnotic voice instead of being angry is that you are calmer and healthier, which means you don't lose seconds off your life that can add up to years over time, and the relationship benefits. Being angry rarely works in a relationship; talking about your anger is more effective.

Another technique that works concurrently with the hypnotic voice to keep your pace healthy is **reverse mirror**. Don't rise to the level of an excited person or group. Do the reverse. What that means is if they speed up—you slow down; if they are overly loud—you soften. You change your voice speed. You slow down your gestures. You ask for time to consider ideas and decisions. You decide the pace at which you want to go, and don't let others decide for you!

There is a third "P" as a result of having more **patience** and purposely changing the **pace** of one's life, and that is **protection**. A definite way to protect your health and well-being is to deal patiently with people's expectations and establish your own boundaries, while at the same time consciously changing the pace of your interactions with others.

For things to be different, you need to be different.

TEETER-TOTTER

If you deal with people who are always calm, even-tempered, and cooperative, there is no need for a strategy to communicate with them. You just discuss things rationally and reasonably. However, in the real world, we have to deal with irrational, moody, and angry people who come at us wanting to get their own way. It occurs to me that our response, to have an impact on them, needs to be the opposite of what they are expecting (see **reverse mirror** in P + P = P, page 6).

I recall from my teeter-totter days as a kid that when I was either up or down, I used a lot of energy to get back to a balanced position. The balanced, static position is really the starting point and once in that position, we use the least energy. So it is with communication. The balance point is where we experience the most success in discussing, understanding, and negotiating. Things just seem to flow better when in balance.

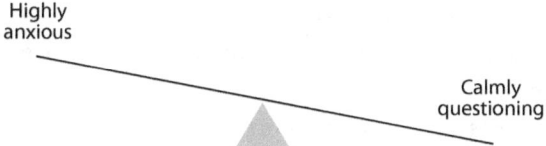

To deal with irrational, moody, and angry people, use the technique of meeting their extremes with calmness. This helps bring them down to a calmer state rather than triggering their anxiety and escalating the instability. Use your quiet, calm, hypnotic voice to contrast the anxiety and anger of the other person.

When emotions are high, you are low. If they are depressed, you are hopeful. If they are sad, you are uplifting. If they are anxious, you are calm. If they are angry, you are understanding. In this way, you invite the other person to move into a static position and the chances of hearing each other are considerably improved.

TODAY A CHOICE, TOMORROW A LIFESTYLE

Behavior, or what we actually do, comes from the ability and the right to make a choice. We can choose to work out or not work out.

I can phone somebody that I need to phone or choose not to phone them. Pay bills or not pay bills. None of this is extremely profound, but it is interesting, particularly if we understand that many people don't feel they have the ability, right, or opportunity to make choices. Even if I don't consciously use my power and right to choose, I am still choosing. *To choose to do nothing is still a choice.*

I've discovered that if I don't make a conscious choice to do or not do something in three consecutive days—if I just let it go, or if I procrastinate in making a choice—I am, in effect, still making a choice for a different kind of lifestyle. Can I choose not to go for a walk today? Sure, it's a choice, but it's not a lifestyle change. My lifestyle can still include walking. The second day, can I choose not to go walking? Yes, because I still haven't taken walking out of my lifestyle. However, if on the third day I choose not to go walking, I have made a commitment, a definite move into the area of changing a lifestyle.

So, do we want the choice of not working out on a certain day or eating a piece of chocolate cake every once in a while or just relaxing and not driving ourselves so hard on certain days? Yes! But I warn you…be careful what you choose, because as innocent, pleasant, or necessary as it may seem, before you know it, in just **three days**, it can become a permanent **lifestyle change**.

It is also important for you to remember that when making changes, what you **start** doing is more important than what you **stop** doing (see *Change,* page 13).

Remember—three consecutive days begins a new lifestyle habit.

CONSCIOUS VS. AUTOMATIC

I don't trust myself, and others even less, when it comes to automatically making good lifestyle choices.

I believe people store messages on their brain computers that cause them to make automatic choices that may be detrimental to their health:

- work until the job is done, then you can play
- if you want something done, do it yourself
- if it's worth doing, it's worth doing well—all the time

These messages are essentially concerned with perfectionism and, if followed consistently, will rob us of our health.

A lot of learned behaviors (messages) are automatic in that we do them without conscious thought. To get our lives in balance requires us to remain focused, to stay on track, and to think daily about what we need to do to achieve our goals. We need to stay in the **here and now** and make decisions consciously, not based on old habits.

You need to think and plan more consciously about what is healthy and good for you, instead of just responding to what you **should do**. Perhaps you have already started…

Perfection is most often a dysfunctional state.

Other people don't need to be different for me to get healthy.
In fact, I expect them to remain the same.
What I do need to change is me, and I will—
right after the crisis.

STARTING OVER

I just get in shape, and I injure my leg. I just get on a roll eating appropriately and it's Thanksgiving. Don't lose heart, just get up tomorrow and start over. After all: life is just a series of "starting-over"!

This is my premise and if you buy into it—read on! Quite often, change is about forming new, positive habits. A **habit** can become ingrained into your life by performing that action for three consecutive days. Once the habit is incorporated into your life, missing a day or two, at most, is not a guilt problem. We can miss up to two days guilt-free before we need to be overly concerned, to refocus and to get back on track. For example, if we exercise vigorously, it can be a good idea to miss a day or two after several intense workouts to give the body a chance to recover. It does not mean that we are starting over. It is not until we miss the third day that we are starting a new habit that may not be positive. Missing a day or two on purpose or because of illness is no big deal, as long as we get back at it for the next three days. We need to give ourselves permission to stop pushing ourselves, to go off our diet for a day, to accomplish little for a day, to miss a workout or two because we just don't feel like it, and we need for it to be guilt-free.

Don't beat yourself up—just get up tomorrow and **start over.**

Life is just a series of "starting-over."

PERMISSION TO TRY NEW THINGS

One definition of insanity is "doing the same thing over and over and expecting a different outcome."

Clients who subscribe to a philosophy that is clearly not working often express statements such as these:

> "I am depressed, my life is absolutely no fun; I just seem to work harder each year and have less time for myself."

They have been programmed to believe they need to "just work harder and things will take care of themselves." No, working harder at something that clearly isn't working certainly won't fix the problem.

Think about the following:

- If you keep doing what you're doing, you'll keep getting what you're getting!
- Figure out what works and do more of it!
- Figure out what doesn't work and do less of it!
  (*Options for Solution Focused Therapy*)

We need to give ourselves permission to try new things, even if we don't know what the outcome will be. We need to give up some of the precious control in our lives and just change some things. *See what happens, rather than try to control what happens.* On the other hand, change doesn't always mean better, but neither has maintaining the status quo, especially when we already know what doesn't work.

We sometimes need to go against what we have come to believe is the best way of doing things and find newer, healthier ways of living our lives.

There is some inexplicable and unavoidable logic in the saying: "Sometimes we need to lose our mind to come to our senses."

The only thing I know for sure about change, besides being inevitable, is that we will at least **feel alive** when we have tried something new, or done something old in a different way.

BETTER

The theme for several sessions with a client was, "I can't really do anything to help myself because I am depressed."

I believe that if you change your behavior to something more positive, positive feelings will follow.

As a result of this discussion about **change** and doing something **different** came a new slant—the concept of **Better**. We need to work on making things better, or they get worse!

We need to continually work at making our lives better. We don't always get better but we need to strive, to have goals that will at least allow for the possibility. We don't just do activities because it is "nice" or we "should." We do things, activities, because they contribute to our quality of life.

Making things "better" might look like getting in shape, purchasing a new piece of furniture, acquiring a new skill, or learning to be more assertive.

Life has an attritional aspect to it; it wears us down, and invites us to feel depressed. Sometimes we need to work at "better" just to stay even, to not be depressed.

Work at making your life "better"
or do nothing and run the risk of it getting worse.

Scratching an itch feels good,
but if you keep scratching the same place
(doing the same thing over and over),
you'll create a sore.

CHANGE

When starting the "change process,"
it is not what you stop doing that is most important,
but rather what you start doing!

It seems that when people want to make changes in their lives, they generally start by wanting to eliminate a bad habit, such as overeating, drinking too much, or smoking. What they end up doing is concentrating on that which they are saying they could live without (i.e., the bad habit). I believe long-term success is best achieved by focusing on the actual **behavior you want** rather than what you don't want. For example, decide to establish a sensible eating plan as opposed to not eating sweets anymore. Start a fitness plan rather than focusing on stopping drinking and smoking.

It's true that stopping poor lifestyle habits is important. However, there is more to be gained if you first decide what you want to have happen. Start the positive process; then it will be easier to stop bad habits—permanently—if there is no vacuum to fill.

Our ability to change is both limited and limitless,
depending on our level of self-esteem.

If you keep doing what you're doing,
you'll keep getting what you're getting.

UNDERSTANDABLE BUT NO LONGER APPROPRIATE

As people told me their life stories, I came to understand there were real and rational reasons for their choices in behavior. Going back over their histories, it becomes evident that people make the best choices they can under the particular circumstances in which they find themselves.

Very young children don't have real choices in regards to personal power or rational decision-making skills. Often they develop survival skills, and if we look at their family of origin, the community in which they grew up, the time period of their growing up, and geographical location, their behavior is understandable. But as adults, they realize these behaviors are no longer appropriate.

It seems we keep doing things in the same old way—even when it no longer works—because it made sense in our family of origin or it "used to work." Adults do have the power to choose, to reason, to confront, to make things different. However, many didn't and couldn't when they were children, and so they learned how to survive without the power they now have as adults.

There's no need to continue to overwork at the expense of one's health just because earlier in life that person learned not to deal with unhappy feelings, feared confrontation, or agonized that somebody might not like them. One immerses oneself in work instead of dealing with those anxieties at that time. Adults have the power to deal with their feelings and to rationally know that people won't dislike them and leave them if they do not please them all the time.

Do you exhibit behaviors or feelings that make sense in light of your background—i.e., afraid to get close to people because of a hurtful childhood—but feel the need to change now that you are an adult? Do you now realize you have the personal power to make the changes and do what makes the most sense for a powerful, rational thinking adult?

*My behavior is "understandable,"
but no longer "appropriate."*

SYSTEMS DON'T LIKE TO CHANGE

I am not going to try to define what "systems" are, but merely acknowledge their existence. Couples, families, communities, teams, and workplaces are examples of systems. Affect one part of a system and it shows up in another part. Systems are interdependent.

My observation has been that systems develop and evolve behaviors—ways of dealing with issues that become very consistent. To change these responses is not easy, or in many cases, not considered desirable. Interestingly, even when a behavior is not working well, or when people, events and times have changed significantly to warrant altering, the **system** wants to keep on doing things in the same old way—it **resists change**.

Many parents want to impose their values on the family system in the same way their parents did to them. It doesn't work, but that doesn't stop them from repeating the same behavioral message over and over, eliciting the same negative responses. The same thing happens at the school worksite. Educators apply the same methods they have always used, even though these methods don't work with today's kids, kids who fight back rather aggressively.

We need to change, but our personal systems do not change easily; we do not like to get into unfamiliar, uncharted waters. **Change** unfortunately often occurs only when we are pushed, when we are forced through illness or traumatic events to examine ourselves and explore new ways of dealing with old issues.

It is time to embrace change, open up, see other possibilities, ideas, and methods, and not wait until change becomes a "have to."

What the mind can conceive, you can achieve.

IF IT ISN'T WORKING, CHANGE IT!

"What should I change—my life, job, relationship? I don't like my life, but what should I change and how should I change it?"

I've heard these questions many times over the years. Mostly, I don't have a satisfactory answer. I don't know what you have tried, so I don't know what to suggest that would be "different" for you. What possibilities do you see? Is your self-esteem level high enough, your "pot" full enough, to go out on a limb and change something?

What do you mean by change? The way you talk to people? The way you see your life; your eating, exercise, and sleep habits? Change from a pessimist to an optimist, from a cup-half-empty to a cup-half-full person? Change your routines at home? I don't know the details of what you should change in your life to feel more fulfilled, but you do. Is it about time to consider some changes?

When you first start changing things, it probably isn't so important **what** you change as it is that you are **open** to change. All big changes start with one small step, and small adjustments are the building blocks of sustained change.

We usually don't embrace change until we are absolutely forced to do so through a critical incident such as illness, the threat of a relationship ending, or a pink slip at work. Apparently, **change** is something to be resisted, avoided, and feared, rather than accepted and embraced as a natural part of the process of life. We hang on to doing whatever it is we do in the same old way until we no longer have the energy to continue, or forces prevent us from continuing in the same way.

A member of one of my support groups had a strong point when he stated, "I will continue as I always have, and consider changing only when I can no longer continue, when there is no more fight in me, and when I am too fearful."

It's too bad we have to hit a crisis before we can embrace the possibility of living our lives differently!

GOOD STUFF JOURNAL

Quite different from ordinary journal writing is the kind where you write only about the good stuff in your life, hence the name **good stuff journal**. I often ask clients to record at the end of the day those things they did or said which indicate to them that they are on the right track to making good decisions about their health and taking care of themselves.

Too often what are written in journals are traumatic events in daily lives, which have little to do with improving one's life and health.

Don't deny positive events. Take time and energy to write about them. It's worth it. Let's emphasize only those things we want to continue to have happen. Let's write about the **good stuff**, stuff we feel good about. Recording and commenting about what we are doing is the first step toward seeing that behavior repeated.

Keeping a good stuff journal just might be one of the activities you need to help you stay on track for whatever behavior you want to change and/or maintain.

Taking care of yourself needs to be
a lifelong commitment because you are
probably going to live long enough
to wish that you had.

(inspired by Mark Twain)

ENERGY

I do not purport to be an expert on the human energy system. However, I believe that the human body is quite capable of producing enough energy to carry us right through our workday, and still have enough at the end of the day for a "Real Life." Energy is not like having 10 lbs. of butter—use 2 lbs. up and you only have 8 lbs. left. **Human energy is boundless.** The more we do, the more excited we are, and the more energy we produce.

We run out or run down because of blockages in the pathways in the body that interfere with the flow of energy. These blocks are negative beliefs or thoughts. For example, "I have to be home early to get my eight hours of sleep or I can't function the next day" is translated to "I shouldn't have fun on a school/work night because I will use up the supply of valuable energy and it won't be available for the next day." After all, work should be the focus and purpose of your life…uh, no!

The body's energy does not get used up, but rather is blocked by certain beliefs of the mind. I can play tennis or talk to a good friend until midnight and still get up at the same time the next morning actually feeling more alive. I believe we don't use up energy by doing what we like to do, but we actually start energy flowing.

Energy systems are jump-started by **activities and people** of our choice because we perceive them to be positive. We don't use energy up when we play cards, take a class on stained-glass art, or do aerobics. We somehow clear the energy pathways and more energy flows, and is still accessible the next day for the activity of living. We need to give ourselves permission to identify and do activities often, with individuals of our choosing.

During those times when you are into saving your energy for the "shoulds" and "have tos," ask others how they perceive you regarding your energy and attitude toward life. Feedback will no doubt show that you are much **more alive** when you choose to do fun activities with positive people, rather than have to do things like work and "duty" activities.

TO FEEL GOOD REQUIRES ENERGY

It's my contention that we can get through a day using minimal energy. We can even be sick and survive the day. However, if we plan to have fun, be enthusiastic, and enjoy life, we will need twice as much energy as we would to just get through the day.

We need a plan, a lifestyle, a consistent set of behaviors that will allow us to rejuvenate our body's energy. We need a very healthy body and mind to feel good. Acquiring that is no accident; we need a **plan**.

Feeling good, having energy at the end of a busy workday, doesn't just happen. We need to actually do something to ensure the continuation of good feelings.

Good feelings flow from a well-balanced lifestyle. We so easily delude ourselves into believing that good feelings will continue, despite how we treat ourselves. Because it requires energy, the hard part is choosing to do healthy things consciously, continuously, and on purpose.

Balance is the key to a healthy lifestyle.

Your feelings today are a result of how you treated yourself three months ago. Taking pills has an effect on you that is almost immediate; however, if you want to be healthy (and stable without any kind of medication) this means exercise, proper nutrition, the right amount of sleep, networking, and lots of laughter. To get healthy naturally will take considerably more time and energy. So, what you do and how you treat yourself today will be reflected in your health three months from now.

QUIET ENERGY

The premise is that when you rid your body of tension by taking a brisk walk for 5–10 minutes or doing other positively perceived activities, your body doesn't use up energy, but instead frees up more energy from within.

Tense energy is still good energy, like the kind that propels the frenetic "Type A" personalities. However, there is a different kind of energy, one that is healthier and more productive. It is **quiet energy** that allows the individual to work at a calm, relaxed pace, longer and healthier.

How does one tap into their quiet energy? Exercise is certainly a basic stress reducer when done consistently. Meditation clears the mind of anxiety and produces thoughts that ease muscle tension, as does getting one's life in order. Positive mental thoughts, daydreaming, and fantasizing help to relax tension in the body. Hot baths, massage, reflexology, and deep breathing all allow the body to tap into quiet energy.

Quiet energy accessed through relaxing the body is much like a golf swing. The more relaxed the body is on impact with the ball, the more energy is directly transferred to the spot of impact, and the ball goes further. In the same way, the more relaxed the body is in a work situation, project or crisis, the more energy becomes available to it, and the longer and healthier the body can perform.

Life does not stop having its funny moments
just because bad things happen to good people. Inversely,
life does not cease to be serious when we are laughing.

LIFE FORCE VS. LIFESTYLE ENERGY

A concept I've borrowed from Hans Selye, the Canadian stress researcher, is his idea of **Life Force Energy**. Life Force Energy is different than day-to-day energy. It is the reserve when regular energy, which is fueled by a healthy lifestyle, is depleted. It is the essence, the soul, the last bastion of our energy. However, this source of energy is finite in that just so much of it is available to us, and when we use it up we get very sick, often give up and die.

I don't know the actual chemistry of this energy. I only know I've experienced it when I have pushed myself too hard for too long a time and I have had to reach down inside me and steel myself to do the task at hand. Apparently, we can only reach down and use this life force energy so many times before it gets depleted and we get sick.

I believe we need to establish a way of life that assists us in producing energy, a lifestyle that creates energy, passion, and purpose for life, so we don't have to use the body's life force energy for daily living. We need the life force energy to fight off disease, tragedy, and extreme stress. The life force energy is definitely not to be used for daily living.

A healthy lifestyle is much like the alternator of a car. The alternator provides the energy to produce the spark to drive the pistons on a regular basis. The battery is used only for one moment to start the car. Once the engine is started, the alternator is responsible for the energy to continue driving the engine.

So it is with a properly **balanced lifestyle**. Only occasionally should the body dip into its life force energy, because the way the person has chosen to live life produces the excitement, purpose, and passion—in essence, the energy—to drive that person. Often I hear people saying they wish they had more energy. To have more energy and pour it into a lifestyle that is without balance is to waste that energy. I believe what they need is a lifestyle overhaul.

Examining and overhauling your own lifestyle as often as you have your car checked would be intelligent maintenance.

IT'S NEVER TOO LATE TO HAVE A HAPPY CHILDHOOD

In my job as a therapist, I see people every day with a hurt, scared little person trapped inside. This child (C) has not had the opportunity in their family to do those things that little children do naturally when they are adequately nurtured. Instead, they have learned dysfunctional behaviors to help them survive.

The essence of a child is pure feeling. In a family where abuse is perpetrated on family members, the child, who is either the victim of or a witness to the abuse, is often forced early in life to be responsible for self-survival. This is also typical when a member of the family is alcoholic. The child learns certain grown-up survival behaviors, and while they do survive, they miss out on the opportunity for a happy childhood.

Children raised in dysfunctional families often have to be little adults (A), figuring out how to keep themselves safe at a very early age. They never really have the opportunity to be a child—a fun-loving, curious, creative, mischievous, wonderfully naive, little human being.

I think it is very important for individuals to know they have done the best they can, and that they be praised for surviving. Rational thinking does not usually develop until around age 12, so the child has to decide how to make sense of the craziness that confronts them before they actually have the ability to make sense of it.

If nurtured properly by the adults early in their life, the natural task for the child is to develop a sense of humor, spontaneity, curiosity, creativity; in essence, to be a fun-loving person, not solely in charge of keeping themselves safe. Safety is normally considered the responsibility of the adults in this young person's life. After the age of 12, their own rational thought process naturally takes over that task.

According to family communication experts Satir and Bradshaw, almost everybody comes from a dysfunctional family. If this is correct, then it is all the more important for each of us to accept that we come from a dysfunctional family with dysfunctional coping behaviors.

Perhaps that is the reason why many of us:

- are so focused on work,
- feel a need to control most events and people in our lives,
- have fears and nightmares of our family of origin, and
- exhibit such driven behaviors.

Our "child" has been forced to be an adult before its time, has not been allowed to play, and is still in urgent need of a happy childhood.

We could start by figuring out what's fun for the "child," what tastes good, what colors are fun, and what activities make us giggle. And we could embark on the search for a happy childhood by making friends with small kids who can show us the way. If they are not readily available, then we can be friends with those grown-ups who already have a strong, fun child inside them.

It's never too late to have a happy childhood.

I can't make you learn.
I can't make you behave.
I can only reach out and invite you to…

I respect the "hard lessons" in life, like loss and failure.
However, I don't focus on them for too long because I need to
get on with the positive excitement of life to stay healthy.

If it is true that everyone comes from a
dysfunctional family, then you are just "normally"
screwed up and not "specially" screwed up.

PROJECT VS. TIME THINKING

*I started painting my fence at 6:00 p.m. At 9:45,
I hung lights so I could finish the job by midnight.
I didn't get to go for my run, I didn't play with my kids,
I didn't have tea with my wife, I missed my favorite comedy on TV,
and I didn't phone my best friend.
However, I did finish the painting project.*

A great many of us are what I like to call **project thinkers**. We think along the lines of completing a project without considering how much time it takes or what important health behaviors might be ignored. The sole focus is completing the project.

A small paragraph in *Reader's Digest* about one of the most successful authors of our time convinced me there was another way to look at time, a better way than "project thinking." The author starts work at 10:00 a.m. and at the 12-noon cuckoo, he shuts off his computer, mid-sentence, and goes down to the beach on the Mediterranean. At first, I discounted this behavior and found the paragraph quite ridiculous. After all, whom did I know that started work at 10:00, finished at noon, and went to a Mediterranean beach? However, after returning to this short paragraph many times, something became imminently clear to me—I was a project thinker.

Similarly, I was reading about a person who viewed his day as having a certain and determined number of hours and he continually chose how to use this time. Like the successful author, this guy was a **time thinker**, the concept of which was quite foreign to me because I come from a long line of project thinkers. If it took 15 minutes or six hours, I would see it through to completion, giving absolutely no thought to personal or familial wellness. My priorities in life were totally focused on projects. This scenario plainly didn't work, because I nearly burned out.

There are other ways to live. You can choose how much time you spend at work and play. You can shift your paradigm enough so that you work to time and learn to set boundaries. You can choose how you use time rather than be directed by projects, which is simply another word for work.

WORK VS. REAL LIFE

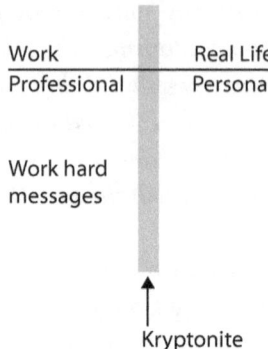

When I first began researching stress and time management, I simplistically saw my life as slotted into two major compartments—my professional life and my personal life. Much time has passed, but I still believe in the compartmentalization idea; however, years of experience have taught me that it's not my actual profession alone that will burn me out and result in harmful symptoms, as I had originally thought. It is in fact a preoccupation with work, whether on the job or at home, from which I need to protect myself. It became clear to me that far too many "work hard" messages had been passed down from generation to generation in my family. The "Rosin" addiction to work was at the root of the burnout, and not the job or the profession itself.

I have always believed that it's not what you stop doing that is most important, but rather what you start doing. So, if I am to remain true to my own beliefs, then it's not the cutting down on work that will be most helpful to your health, but rather focusing on the components of a healthy life—a **Real Life**.

Eventually, I realized that in my original compartmentalization idea, the concept of a "personal life" was inadequate. **Real Life** implies that one's "personal life" is more important than their "professional life," and more quality time and energy should be invested in the personal side of one's life. I am convinced that a commitment to a Real Life is a must for individuals to be physically and psychologically healthy.

In your life, you need to work but you also need a Real Life to be in balance. People and activities in your Real Life ought to be the priority.

A, B, OR C PILE – YOU CHOOSE!

When attempting to make changes in your life so that more of your time and energy is directed to fun and relaxation and less to work, you had better figure out what is really necessary in terms of work and what is habitual or driven behavior.

Here are three good lines I've heard over the years about how to determine what is really necessary and important so I know how much time and energy to devote to work:

- "If I looked at this problem/situation a year from now, how much real effect would it have had on me?"
- "Is this situation life threatening? Then how come I am treating it like it is? And worrying like it is?"
- "Why treat a 10-cent problem with a 10-dollar solution?"

In the field of time management, they talk about piling the paper that comes across your desk every day in three piles:

- **Pile A** — things that have to be done that day
- **Pile B** — things that could wait a day or two
- **Pile C** — things that will get done someday

The suggestion that I heard was to get as much of the paper as possible into Piles B and C. The thinking is that you clear away as much of the paper and details from today so you can:

- get to the really important things, such as people, and
- have enough time and energy left at the end of the workday to seek out fun and relaxing activities in your **Real Life**.

Many of the "mundane details" where you spend the majority of your time and energy are more habitual than necessary. Perhaps you need to rethink your choices regarding how you structure your day, how and to what you respond when crises seem to be reappearing several times a day in the form of paper and people. Is it possible for crises to become the norm? And during a crisis, it is quite impossible to control your time and energy because of that crisis. Right?

Do you let the system and your own habitual way of dealing with things control your choices? Or, do you treat everything like the proverbial "10-dollar problem," thereby having to cover all the bases all the time?

Do you keep everything in Pile A, trying very hard to keep up with all the details and important issues simultaneously? Or, do you start making some hard choices, having determined that you have options? Do you then begin to set some firm boundaries to choose what is really important? Do you prioritize, accept and act as if there is a need for **balance**, with the understanding that all things can't be dealt with immediately?

Some days your desk will not be cleared, everything will not be completed. This will then enable you to have **time** and **energy** left for **a Real Life**.

Tension robs the body of energy.
Relaxation allows the body to make available
energy at a high rate for an extended period of time.

Replace the old picture of yourself
(i.e., working all the time, perfectionist, serious minded)
with a healthy new one
(i.e., happy, free, independent, risk-taker, fun-loving).

KISS THE BRICKS GOODBYE (THANKS, DONALD MEICHENBAUM)

Leave your work at work.

You have to take your driver's license with you when you drive. Some people want to take their money with them when they die. But nobody wants to take their job with them when they leave the workplace!

It truly is impossible to **kiss the bricks goodbye** if your job is your life. Human behavior specialist Donald Meichenbaum's advice is only possible if we are not married to the job and truly understand the meaning of the concept "Get a Life!" A starting point in being able to kiss the bricks goodbye is for you to have a **Real Life** to go to.

If you can spend a perfectly useless afternoon in
a perfectly useless manner, you have learned how to live.
(Emerson)

THE KEY HOUR FOR EVENING ENERGY

I discovered the Key Hour when I was in my 60's (slow learner). After 40 years in the workplace, I finally learned the simple importance of having energy left at the end of the workday. What I've learned is that there is a key to having energy in the evening for your "Real Life." Oh sure, you need to eat right, exercise, take breaks at lunchtime, network with your friends through the day, laugh lots, give and receive love, not have any overpowering events happen too consistently and, of course, you must learn to "kiss the bricks goodbye" at the end of the workday. Along with all of these, one needs to know about the **key hour**.

I don't care how hard I work during the day. If I'm still at work at 6:00 p.m., the evening is shot. In essence then, the **key hour is from 5:00 to 6:00 p.m**. If I choose to end my day at 5:00 p.m., my body has some energy left to propel me into a potentially enjoyable evening. Perhaps this is the necessary energy that will allow me to generate the spice and variety I need to stay healthy.

If I start work early (8-9 am) and I am still at work at 6 pm, this means I get home late and almost right away eat supper. I am usually famished, having waited too long, and so I overeat. Soon it is after 7:00 p.m., and I need to sit for just an hour and rest. Later, I tell myself, I will work on my bike, clean up the workbench, or bottle my wine. My intentions are good, or so I think, but that hour quickly turns into two. Unfortunately, I am now ready to descend into my pre-bedtime relaxation routine, and alas, have no energy for those things I wanted to do. Know what I am talking about?

You might want to consider the time between 5:00 and 6:00 p.m. as a **key energy time** as well. You don't necessarily have to spend it in activity, but use it as a time to finish your workday and use it as a buffer to the rest of your evening and your **Real Life**. A time to drive home, relax, read, joke with the kids, listen to your favorite music, assign supper responsibilities, perhaps even do the cooking, but it should be a different pace to the rest of your day. Be in charge of the 5:00 to 6:00 p.m. time period and you will have more energy for your evening, for your Real Life.

WORK VS. HEALTH MESSAGES

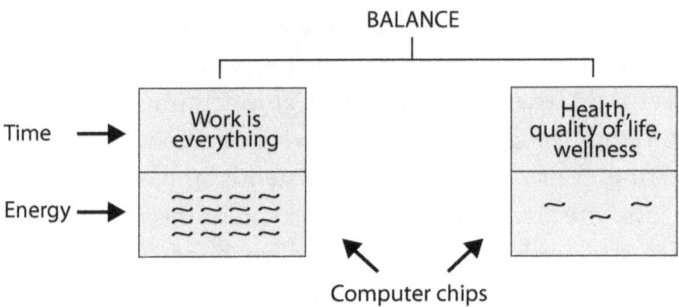

(Located on the brain's computer chip)

It occurred to me one day that a belief I inherited from my family of origin was that "work was the most important thing in my life." This belief was making it very difficult for me to get and stay healthy. Because many of my clients were in their 50s and were definitely having a problem with health and burnout, I assumed this was an age-related issue.

I have since come to understand that burnout is less of a generational condition as it is one of the familial passing on of what I call "messages designed to help you make it in life." For example:

- Work isn't only important, it is everything.
- All problems can be overcome by just working harder.
- You are what you do.

Get the point?

These familial messages that come from our parents, and even from our great, great-grandparents, are positive messages intended to help "make it in life." What I previously didn't understand was that these messages about what is important in life, how we should live our lives, and how we can make it in life are passed on from generation to generation. These messages are our values and beliefs, and what we apparently value most is our ability to work hard.

The problem is that what was important in our lives one or two generations ago is no longer appropriate. Grandpa worked six days a week, 10 hours a day, just to put food on the table. There was no option, no discussion about choice or health. Necessity guided people's work actions in previous generations.

My father worked five days a week at his job with the railway. The other two days, he worked out of the home, gardening and building recreation rooms and concrete pads for other people. This is what he knew, what he understood, to be a good citizen, husband, father, and provider. Like his father, and even though times had changed, he still heard the direction that work is good and necessary: "Not working is wasting time." I heard the same subtle messages, although actually not that subtle at times: "Are you playing ball again? When are you going to finish with that nonsense?"

I grew up feeling like I should be working most of the time. I never understood until I was almost burned out at 40 that I did have an option, and that while **work was good, so was play**. There needed to be a **balance** between the two. What I also learned was that it was very hard for people in their late 40s and older to change their behavior and include more fun and relaxation in their daily lives. It wasn't because they were slow or didn't have the desire to change, but because they did not have **permission** to do so. They didn't have many health messages on the computer chip in their brain to play, relax, and take care of themselves. As a result, workers who do not lead a balanced lifestyle eventually get frustrated, resentful, and burned out. It is not easy to start creating messages that give permission to take better care of self, but that is exactly what we must do.

I would encourage you to re-examine the decision that has you continuing to make work a priority in your life. Consider the difference if you chose a balanced lifestyle that supports **wellness and quality of life** instead of more work.

Your choice!

After me and my family, you're first.

EGO VS. HEALTH

As I have stated many times, I believe that here in North America, we are not really programmed during infancy to take responsibility for our health. I believe there is an over-dependency on doctors. I believe people too often say "I will take it easy" or "I will get in shape some day but for today, career and kids have a much higher priority than personal health choices." As well there is another factor that gets in the way of making good health decisions, and that quite simply is **ego**.

As I see it, ego is not all that bad, if it isn't the expanded-head kind. My way of looking at ego says, for example, I like to look my best. I'll cut my grass and paint my house because it looks good. I like to be known as a good person with some class and so I keep things shipshape. This is a **healthy ego**.

However, it is easy to see that if you carry ego to the point of even mild obsession and focus on your physical to the detriment of your other holistic dimensions, you will become unbalanced and susceptible to burnout. If your ego says I can't be satisfied until I'm the best, no matter what the cost, then ego will continue to take precedence over your health (see *Stand and Deliver*, page 123).

One Sunday morning, the concept of ego-versus-health became crystal clear. I was playing in the final period of an old-timer hockey game, enjoying one of my frequent fantasies about being Wayne Gretzky, when suddenly I found myself face down on the ice, victim of a rather stiff elbow to the back of my head. I scrambled to my knees, about to act on first impulse—"Nobody does that to me and gets away with it!" Pure ego. When I found my legs and started to retaliate, the form of a very, very large man loomed above me...and beyond me.

The concept of ego-versus-health jumped into my mind and I actually laughed, which, by the way, almost always breaks the ego grip and changes your behavior. I went over to the bench with a smile on my face, where none of my teammates were paying any attention to what had happened. None, except for a very good friend and colleague who leaned over and, looking past a few players, mouthed, "Health, eh?"

This humorous incident is a reminder that ego can be extremely detrimental to your health, even in situations far less graphic and potentially physically harmful as the incident on ice.

You need to become aware that you have an ego and it can actually help you keep a positive edge. However, your personal health and the health of your relationships must be a priority. You must exercise discipline—ego must not be allowed to control and direct your life.

*In the same way that ego can direct one's life,
so can the drive for accomplishment and success.
There will always be a reason to work longer and harder,
to be unbalanced, rather than to take care of one's own health.*

*You can't be held responsible for what pops into your
mind (i.e., worry, thoughts, feelings), but you are
responsible for what comes out of your mouth.*

SLURP IT UP

If I had my life to live over...

*If I had my life to live over, I'd dare to make more mistakes next time.
I'd relax. I'd limber up. I would be sillier than I was this time.
I would take fewer things seriously. I would take more chances.
I would take more trips. I would climb more mountains and swim more
rivers. I would eat more ice cream and less beans. I would perhaps
have more actual troubles, but I'd have fewer imaginary ones.*

*You see, I am one of those people who live sensibly and sanely,
hour after hour, day after day. Oh, I've had my moments, and
if I had it to do over again, I'd have more of them. In fact,
I'd try to have nothing else, just moments, one after another,
instead of living so many years ahead of each day.*

*I've been one of those persons who never goes anywhere without
a thermometer, a hot water bottle, a raincoat, and a parachute.
If I had it to do over again, I would travel lighter than I have.
If I had my life to live over, I would start barefoot earlier in the spring
and I would stay that way later in the fall. I would go to more dances.
I would ride more merry-go-rounds. I would pick more daisies.*

A great many people live their life as if it were in a **black-and-white** film, devoid of **color**—little excitement, limited choices, minimal fun, taking few risks, very predictable, having no edge, and certainly no gusto.

The poem by 86-year-old Nadine Satir clearly announces that if given a second chance, she would live her life very differently. I think she speaks for many of us.

Many of us are missing the banquet that life has provided.

We see only the neutral to negative side of life. Maybe next time, as Satir states, we could live life a little less safely and add a bit more color to it. We could choose to see life as an opportunity to be lived fully, rather than a place where we need to survive. "Thank God it's Friday" seems to be our declaration of survival. We need to **slurp** out the color, the excitement that life offers. We need to be willing to take a chance, to risk losing what is, before the color will come back into our lives.

Think of today as your second chance.

> *How can you slurp up the excitement of life in technicolor when you're choosing to live in the mundane black-and-white details of life?*
>
> *We need to have a vision; we need to know what a balanced person or lifestyle looks like before we can change and "do" that behavior.*

STEW JUICE

Don't stew—state!

When you hold on to a feeling or a thought and keep it inside you instead of speaking from your mind or heart, you stew. Stewing for two or three days instead of stating your principles—thoughts, feelings, values, and beliefs (T F V B)—will not only have you feeling less successful, off-balance, and sick, but will also affect those around you (see *Be Married...*, page 53). Stewing makes everyone sick!

It is much healthier to speak out. State your principles. Deal with other people's responses to your thoughts and feelings. That is certainly preferable to anticipating their upheaval, flak, and/or anger. By keeping quiet, you end up stewing.

Success:
the degree to which you state your mind,
are congruent, are at peace with the world,
and know about love!

Take care of yourself first
so you can take better care of others.

DON'T STEW – DO!

*This is what I should do! What I have to do!
I have no options!*

We think and analyze far too much in our lives. It stops us from doing things. Anger, frustration, and fear tapes are played over and over in our heads, but nothing comes out of our mouths. We think about our feelings rather than express them, thereby keeping them trapped in our heads. This becomes negative headspace and, like poison, soon begins to permeate the physical body. Eventually, our total health is affected (emotional, intellectual, work, spiritual, physical, social).

The poem written by 85-year-old Nadine Satir (see *Slurp It Up*, page 36) declares that if she were to do it over again, "I would perhaps have more actual troubles, but I'd have fewer imaginary ones." The poem states that **real issues and problems are part of life**. While it is not good to deny that, living in our heads, making up and magnifying problems and issues is also very destructive. A lot of energy is used to deny or cover up our negative thoughts or feelings. If instead we used that energy to design a **plan of action** to work out the problems, we would accomplish more, be far healthier, and still have energy left over for living the positives.

There is something to that old adage, "When it comes to problems—do something, design a plan, or let it go." I totally agree.

Do or do not. There is no trying.

FINDING BALANCE | 39

PLAY ISN'T NICE – IT'S IMPERATIVE

My wife and I often go to the movies as a way of relaxing and coping with the stress in our lives. We were standing in the foyer of a downtown theatre when an acquaintance spotted me and came over. Foot tapping and hands on hips—a somewhat judgmental pose—he asked me how I could possibly be at the movies when he had "…heard you were so busy." He must have been referring to the waiting list of clients we often have when working in an Employee Assistance Program (EAP). "Must be nice." I wished he hadn't said that.

My response to him was quite unexpected to all within hearing distance. I shouted almost at the top of my lungs and he backed away. "Nice? You think it's nice coming to this movie theatre, eating popcorn, holding my wife's hand, laughing, enjoying ourselves?" Immediately putting an "I-don't-know-this-fool" look on her face, my wife, and his, made a dash for the restroom.

It was then I realized how strongly I felt about the necessity of play in taking care of self. Being at the movies isn't only nice; it's a must, a requirement. **Play** is more than nice; it is absolutely **imperative** for a healthy life. Play is a condition of life, like breathing, eating, working. Our wives did come back, slowly accepting us as two guys they knew. However, I believe it will be a long time before my acquaintance suggests to anybody that play is merely "nice."

Did you know that **play**—relaxation, enjoyment—was in the same "league" (health wise) as breathing and eating? Well, now you do! You may not feel as strongly about it as I do, but the more you apply this notion of play being imperative in our lives, the potentially healthier you will become. How healthy? That's up to you!

Work is what you do in between play times.

PLANNED SPONTANEITY

Yes, planned spontaneity is an oxymoron. However, to a person with a "Type A" or "workaholic"-type personality, planned spontaneity is key to unlocking and breaking "the work hard" cycle. **Plan for fun.**

Plan to participate in a fun time and when you show up at the activity, you will most likely be more spontaneous.

I know this about most people—get them into an environment where others are enjoying themselves and having fun, and shortly they will too. It is unproductive to try to teach people to have fun. Rather, get them to commit to attending potentially fun events and activities.

A plan is necessary so we will do things, get out to events, network with others, and visit exciting places. Spontaneous fun will then take care of itself. The plan will result in spontaneity.

If we better understood that fun and relaxation are absolutely essential for a healthy and well-balanced life, then we might allow ourselves more time to do those things. If we wait for the spontaneity to lead us to enjoyable times, we will remain starved. Instead, plan fun like you plan work, and you might find yourself spontaneously breaking into a healthy laugh or whistle.

> *Listen to your life. See if for the fathomless mystery that it is.*
> *In the boredom and pain of it, no less than in the excitement*
> *and gladness: touch, taste, smell your way to the holy*
> *and hidden heart of it because in the last analysis,*
> *all moments are key moments, and life itself is grace.*
> *(Frederick Buechner)*

SPICE IS A NECESSITY FOR A BALANCED LIFESTYLE

Spice isn't just nice—it's imperative!

The word "spice" was coined by Hans Selye to emphasize the necessity of having variety in our lives. Like Selye, I believe that to be physically and psychologically healthy, to be in balance, an individual needs to be open to a variety of activities and experiences. From Selye, I understand that spice or variety is the relief the body needs from sameness. We interpret difference as excitement and aliveness, and we feel more worthwhile and more in charge of our lives. Change has a chemical affect on our bodies, charging it up, but also allowing us to psychologically feel in control. All this works on our self-esteem, one of the most important and powerful determinants influencing overall health.

It's possible that you've been caught up in the work-all-day and work-all-evening way of life. Maybe it's time to examine options that include more variety and spice.

Sometimes overwork is not the killer, but boredom and relentless routine can be.

Be careful what you wish for, because it just may come true.

NEGATIVE THOUGHTS CAN BE CONTROLLED

You can't be held responsible for what pops into your mind—worry, thoughts, feelings—but you can be held responsible for what you do with these thoughts—your behavior.
Dan Rosin

There is such a thing as **learned helplessness**, "victim" behavior that says, "It just comes into my mind and I can't help it. It's not my fault. It just is." End of conversation!

Some people entertain negative thoughts and feelings more often and for longer periods of time than others. Nobody asks for worry-type thoughts, but some people seem to relish replaying negative tapes. Others go for a walk, read a book, or talk to a friend to dissipate the negative thoughts. It reminds me of the saying, "If you have a new idea that will cause you much work, go lie down until it passes."

Instead of lying down when you have a negative thought, train yourself to work out, dance to music, seek out beauty in nature or art, phone a friend, or do something that will be the focus until that thought or feeling passes. It's not busy work but **on-purpose action** that gets you to **refocus** on the positives in your life.

The solution to dealing with negative thoughts or feelings is doing a purposeful activity with the intent of controlling or limiting the amount of time and number of replays of that negative tape.

Inverse paranoia: a person with this condition goes through life believing the world is out to do them good.

WOODY ALLEN

Mr. Allen is a very funny man. Part of his humorous approach is to use self-defacement; in other words, he puts himself down. We, the audience, can identify with that unhealthy way of thinking and acting, and at the same time, find it laughable in some perverse way. I would like to alter one of Mr. Allen's famous lines so that those of you who identify with this particular way of thinking can choose an alternative process. My understanding of this line is: "I find the person who would give me the hardest time in the room, and then I would make my move on them."

I suggest changing the word "hardest" to "best" without undergoing a great deal of therapy. Could we begin to feel better about ourselves if we believed we had a right to spend time with other people who would help us feel good? That we deserved the best time and not the hardest time?

The first step to feeling and believing that we are the best, that we are worthwhile, is to repeatedly say that we are the best. We can feed ourselves positive affirmation-type messages and enact behaviors that are consistent with that feeling and belief. In other words, let's say and do that which is positive, so that we begin to feel and believe that we are the best and that we deserve the best.

Those who worry should focus on doing their best instead of thinking the worst.

NO ME! NO US! ONLY THE PROJECT!

While working with a couple whose livelihood was the performing arts, I referred to their lifestyle, or **workstyle**, as "one project after another." Their projects were a play, a musical, or the writing of a script. As they described their hectic life, it seemed each project had a life of its own, getting all the best time and energy, and taking precedence over prior commitments to self, to each other, to family, to friends. For the life of the project, there was no "me," no "us," no "family" or "friends," only the "project."

When a significant amount of time and one's best energy is invested in a project, it often leaves a person fatigued, with a short attention span, creatively spent, irritable, resentful, and out of balance. After completion, one is emotionally drained, often depressed. How then do you have anything left for a relationship?

Relationships fail when you become exclusively focused on one thing. Soon you begin to feel that your significant other's presence is getting in the way of your next project. **Work** becomes your **life** and there's no room left for anything or anyone else. Many of us treat our occupation, be it teaching, banking, accounting, welding metal, or real estate, in the same manner as the performing arts couple—one project following another to the exclusion of the relationship.

By treating the job as one big project, one event after another, there is no time or quality energy for self or partner. Quite often, however, there is energy for the kids and a whole lot for the job. We need to put the "me" and "us" back into our lives, so as to be healthy and have meaningful relationships. Whether we are in the arts, teaching Grade 4, or selling real estate, we must include in each day the time and energy for: **self, partner, family, friends, and work**. It's called **balance**!

Don't give your best energy away to a series of work projects while the people you care about most are being neglected. Get in "balance" and you will feel a positive difference: a sense of achievement, less obsession with projects, and improved relationships.

WHAT HAPPENED TO THE "WE" IN OUR RELATIONSHIP?

Distancing from your spouse or partner is not difficult. Often a slow process that is hardly noticeable. Where once time was found for a kiss goodbye in the morning, now it is replaced with the scrambling of getting the kids and self out the door to start the workday.

Where once you had a special restaurant you frequented, now you have no money or are too busy chauffeuring young and old in your life to baseball games or medical appointments. In the past bedtime was the time of the day to talk, catch up, and cuddle. Now it's a race to fall asleep first, to get enough sleep to keep up the frenetic pace. Two "I's" passing in the night.

Whoa! Whatever happened to **us** or **we**? If "we" is not worked on regularly, there are often two dissatisfied "I's." Relationships do not just happen and they don't stay healthy without daily maintenance.

Start by thinking "we," and then realize that there is always work to be done on the relationship.

Try sitting side by side—**touching**.

Be a "we" when dealing with problems and people, two **equal partners** dealing with the issue, not necessarily seeing things the same way, but respecting and valuing each other and finding **compromise**. Despite your differences (T F V B), you remain **committed** to the fact that you are a team, a couple, a "we."

Success as a couple takes work.
Are you up to it?

ACTIVE LISTENING

Active listening occurs when the listener focuses on the speaker, using eye contact, appropriate gestures, giving the person their full attention by standing or facing them, and asking questions that indicate they are interested. The speaker feels heard!

Working with couples, I find that poor communication is an identified problem almost 100% of the time. One partner is usually speaking about how they *feel* and the other is paying attention to the *data*. They are talking apples and oranges, with the result that they don't understand the other person. Soon they stop listening to each other altogether. The talking becomes yelling or sarcasm.

Often, one speaks and the other mentally creates a rebuttal, not really listening, or encouraging, but waiting impatiently for the other person to finish so their response can be expressed. Body posture says, "Hurry up. I've something to say that is more important and significant than what you're saying." This bad habit is called **rehearsing**, and is not effective communication.

A second habit that can aggravate and turn people off to the point where they stop communicating is when the listener feels they are supposed to **problem solve**. A high percentage of men who have been encouraged since birth to "cut to the chase" seem to end up problem solving in a relationship. In a majority of instances, the woman has stopped sharing her concerns with him because she doesn't want to be told how to solve her problems, as if she is totally incapable of solving them herself!

Don't ask me how I know this when I can't even figure out the two main women in my own life—wife and daughter—but what a woman wants is to be **understood**, not to have her problems solved for her. Males do problem solving consistently instead of listening, which gets translated into, "He doesn't understand me" or "He thinks I'm stupid."

While on the theme of genders seeing the world differently, I'll make a point for males. We want the **problem solved**. After the second or third discussion of the matter, men aren't all that interested in how you feel about your boss putting you down or being mean to you, but rather will ask, "What're you going to do about it?" If your answer is, "Nothing! I just want you to understand the stress I'm under," he'll probably stop listening. I suggest that if you want to be heard on other issues in the future, then don't bring them up more than twice. You know, three strikes and you're out? Otherwise, there'll be little understanding or sympathy because he'll want the issue solved and for you to move on.

It is true that males and females are different, but we both want to be heard in our own way. The key is to give others our ears and eyes, face them, nod appropriately, and ask questions so that they know they have been heard. **Active listening** is essential to effective communication.

> *The success of active listening is listening to the individual's feelings, not just the content. People "operate" at the intellectual content level, but "live" at the feeling level.*
>
> *Listening means more ears and less mouth.*
>
> *Men listen to solve, women listen to understand. Any problem here?*

LOVE AND NEEDS

The partnership between love and needs became clearer to me during a discussion with a couple. Without any malice or blame they held that, "If you don't help me to meet my needs, then I feel like you don't love me." It seemed that they felt most loved when their needs were being met and their partner was part of that process.

A statistic I read in a book on dating says there are eight people in a six-block area that would be compatible with any individual within that area. This implies that there are a lot of people whom an individual could love. This also raises the question whether it is a particular person or their ability to assist in meeting individual needs that is cherished? Many factors contribute to loving—chemistry, visual cues, and previous history—but research seems to indicate, "you love those who love you."

You love those who show their love for you by assisting you in getting your short and long term needs met. Love that lasts is really about individuals who help each other to meet their needs and are pleased to do that.

Who do you love?
Why those who love me, of course!

COURTESY VS. PERMISSION

Sometimes individuals confuse needing permission from a partner to do something, with just being courteous to the partner. I learned a long time ago I didn't need to ask my wife's permission to take part in the Friday staff meeting at the local pub. But I also discovered if I called and discussed our Friday night plans, to see if they had changed, then she often would be very encouraging about my staying with my colleagues, as well as being supportive when I mentioned golf on Sunday.

My colleagues often made fun of me at the pub because I made that telephone call. They didn't seem to understand (and at that time, I didn't either) that I didn't need **permission** to be there. However, I certainly needed to show some **courtesy** to my partner, which would be rewarded many times over.

Good relationships are not about permission, but rather trust and courtesy.

The "spark" not easily ignited
will often burn the brightest and longest
when overcoming the crisis of daily living.

I don't need your permission to make decisions about my life.
I don't need you to always agree with me.
But I do need you to be courteous and
to respectfully listen to what I have to say.

WELLNESS CONTINUUM

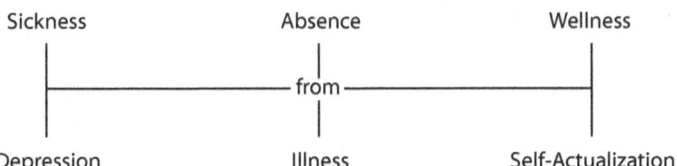

The continuum is not my creation, but I use it consistently with clients and in workshops. It shows the progression from **sickness** to **wellness**. What's most significant is that the majority of the population exists somewhere on the continuum between **sickness** and **absence from illness**. We are satisfied with just not being ill, our goal is to not be ill rather than strive for wellness.

It is common practice for Western medicine to stop service when the patient is not ill. There is a tremendous difference when our goal is to be self-actualized, to be all we can be, entirely healthy and well, as opposed to just being satisfied with not being ill.

It is time to contemplate moving across that midpoint and into the wellness dimension, even if it does take more initial effort, more preparation, more cost. That includes eating right and taking time to plan activities. Perhaps the payoff comes later when you spend less time being ill and create more energy for living.

Wellness is more than the absence of illness.

RELATIONSHIPS AND THE WELLNESS CONTINUUM

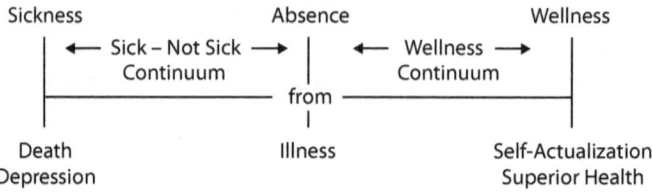

After working with a multitude of couples, it is eminently clear that the *Wellness Continuum* concept (see *Wellness Continuum*, page 51) has as much application for relationships as for wellness.

Many couples describe the quality of their relationship as "not sick" or "not problematic," hence their dialogue emanates primarily in the "sick" to "not sick" dimension. They know their relationship isn't well, it isn't healthy or particularly loving, but it isn't a big problem either. They are willing to settle for "little" rather than challenging the status quo. I have also heard it said by many people that they are willing to live their lives in "quiet desperation"—not happy, but certainly not something they feel they can take charge of and make healthy. Like their own physical health, the relationship "isn't so bad," so they don't put the effort into getting it healthier. They are satisfied with it just "not being sick." A relationship that is only "not sick" isn't enough to keep people together over the long haul.

Relationships will disintegrate over time if not worked on. Relationships grow ↑ or they go ↓.

In relationships, as in personal health, you need to make a more **conscious commitment** to focus and work on changing from sick/not sick language to **wellness/superior health** language.

BE MARRIED TO YOUR PRINCIPLES, BUT NOT THE OUTCOMES

Thoughts	Feelings	Values	Beliefs	
T	F	V	B	Desired
Be Married...				Outcomes

ooooo
(*pearls of wisdom*)

It happened quite innocently one day, when a friend of mine, Gordon, said to me, "Dan, you are going to make yourself sick trying to get them to move where you think they should be." He then quoted a line from a book he had been reading: "Be married to your principles, but not the outcomes."

For a long time, I wasn't fully ready to understand the meaning of that line, but one day while dealing with my rather challenging teenager, Lisa: it became crystal clear to me what those words really meant. It was my mistake to expect that when I discussed with Lisa the issue of her staying out too late—which she really didn't—she would salute me and say, "Of course, Father dear, you are correct and I will be in on time, all the time."

Wow! What planet was I on? I know full well that teenagers, or for that matter most adults, don't operate this way. Despite knowing this, I still felt like a failure when the outcome I fantasized about was not realized, when the desired outcome did not materialize. Back then; I needed the **desired outcome** for me to be a success as a parent. If I didn't get that outcome, I became louder and went on longer in my lectures—and we parents know how well that works.

It was the same on the job. I had ideas and expectations for things to be done in a certain way, and because I did not have the power to control the outcomes, the end result quite often was very different from what I wanted. Once again I felt like a failure.

A breakthrough occurred one morning when I woke up knowing I had to get out of the "outcome" business. What had become clear to me that morning was that I still had to state what I thought, what I felt, what I valued, and what I believed, but I couldn't make or expect people to do what I wanted them to do—the desired outcomes. Their behavior was their choice and really quite beyond my control.

I knew I had to have the freedom to state what was in my heart and on my mind, but not expect a certain outcome because of what I said. I feel strongly about certain things, and I need to give myself permission to state my thoughts, feelings, beliefs and values, but I must not expect individuals to go and do something just because I said it.

The secret revealed to me that morning was that it's imperative to state one's **thoughts, feelings, values, and beliefs** (T F V B) and then let them go, just like the concept of dropping pearls of wisdom. Say what you have to say, but say it in 30 seconds or less (maximum time people will listen anyway). As well, remember to use only "**I**" language because anything else invites defensiveness. Success is in the **stating**, not in the **desired outcome**.

Focus on what is under your control, the feeling of success that comes from being in **charge** of your life, and state what's on your mind and in your heart, rather than being upset about unsuccessful outcomes over which you have no control.

> *I feel a duty to myself and to you to tell you what*
> *I think, feel, value and believe. I don't expect you to act*
> *on what I say or to even like it. However, I hope that you*
> *can help me understand what this means to you.*

APPLYING THE "BE MARRIED" CONCEPT TO DEPRESSION

It is hard to be depressed when one is experiencing success!

Let me explain how the "Be Married…" concept (see page 53) might be helpful in working with depression.

Depression is about not feeling successful, believing that things will never change, a feeling of hopelessness, that "aspirations" will never be achieved. "Life sucks and then you die." One way to simply break this is to feel more successful, to consistently identify the successes in one's life, exert more influence over those things where one does have power instead of focusing on things over which one does not. And sometimes it means taking your medication.

It would be more positive, for example, if a person considered a 15-minute walk a successful thing to do, rather than spend hours stuck in one place trying to design the perfect exercise program. In other words, success can be redefined and measured in small increments, allowing a person to feel more successful more often.

What happens when we focus on the perfect cure instead of a minor success? Quite often we are overwhelmed, and experience a feeling of failure and depression. If I am successful only when I receive total obedience from my teenager, it is inevitable that I will fail, which could contribute to a depressive state. However, if my goal is to speak to that teenager and to share with them, then nobody can take the power of speaking to them away from me, and I will be a success even if I don't influence a change in the teenager's behavior. If walking for 15 minutes a day and eating healthier are my goals, I am "in charge," I can feel the success of doing that daily, and this is what motivates me to continue. Success contributes to one feeling high on life, rather than depressed about it.

We need to understand that it is the courage to **state** where we're at, what we think, feel, value, and believe, that is the goal, the measure of success. We do not have to actually cure the issue—which in most cases is beyond our power—before we can feel successful, before we can feel good about ourselves. We merely have to **state** our position.

Success is in the stating of one's own T F V B, not in changing other people's behavior.

A massage friend of mine taught me to say, "Cancel! Cancel!" whenever I put myself down or talk negatively. Cancel the discontent and then restate it in more positive terms.

Your language, your choice of words, is the lead-in to your behavior. So watch your language!

THE "I," "YOU," AND "WE" LANGUAGE POSSIBILITIES

Talking with a client about the skills necessary to be a good leader led me into some new understanding of the "Be Married…" concept (see page 53).

I had been sharing with a client the idea that "I" language most often resulted in a less defensive listener. Further, when you state your T F V B and not press for an outcome, you come across in a much more positive way and your ideas are accepted more readily. However, there are times when "I" is not appropriate and the use of "you" and "we" are proper.

Being in a relationship requires much "we" and "us" talk. When you are the appointed leader of a group, for example and speaking on behalf of that group, you need to switch from "I" language to "we" language— "we think, feel, value, and believe"—because "we" language is most appropriate.

For example, an individual comes to see me and wants me to present their case to the executive or boss. At that point, it is not a group issue so it is not a "we" issue. A decision has to be made. If I take on this person's issue and speak for them, then it is appropriate for me to use "you" language: "You see it this way?" "You want me to say this for you?" Of course, if I do that, I still have the whole issue of, "Do I take on other people's monkeys?" (see *Stop Collecting Other People's Monkeys*, page 67). As the leader of a group, I am sure that nine out of 10 times, my response would be to place the responsibility back on the other person, and so would likely say, "… and what have you done to solve this issue in the past? How have you seen other people handle this issue?"

There seem to be appropriate times to personalize our language and use "I," to generalize "we," and to place responsibility back on the owner of the problem—"you." Knowing when to use "I," "You," and "We" is essential to good communication.

PANIC ATTACK – FOR WHAT PURPOSE?

I had a client who suffered from severe panic attacks. In fact, he had been devastated to the point of not being able to work. After we had spent an hour examining the extent to which these attacks had taken over his life, it became clear to both of us that they did have a purpose. While we were talking about approaches to dealing with these attacks, I mentioned the **ally theory**. It is believed in some circles that panic attacks are really allies, and are, in some bizarre way, attempting to **protect and help us**. The intent is positive, but the methodology is painful, and the "help" is confusing.

What became clear to us—not necessarily the same as the "truth"—was that panic attacks in this person's case seemed to have something to do with the **issue of control**. We concluded: "If we are not in charge of our life, body, time, pace, and energy, then at some point, some bodily system will remind us, even in a bizarre fashion, to take care of ourselves."

It may be that panic attacks get their direction from the same level of the subconscious that detects when we are not feeling in charge of our lives.

Yes, we did recognize that we had left out the entire **heredity, chemical, and environmental positions** with respect to the cause of panic attacks. Research claims these positions have at least as much validity—actually, considerably more—than our explanation for the purpose of panic attacks, but we liked our explanation better.

And so we stuck to it—the more "in charge" you are of your life, the less often a physical bodily response, a panic attack, will have to remind you to **take charge of your life**.

What does "taking charge" of your life look like?

DECIDE OR OTHERS WILL

More and more, I am beginning to believe that if I don't say what my life will look like, somebody else will.

If I don't say what I want, somebody will say what they want and will expect me to go along with it, seeing as I am not doing anything anyway, they think. If I don't decide what I want to do with my 24 hours each day—the same amount of time everybody else has—then messages/drivers in my own head or other people's head will certainly inform me of what I should and have to do.

Most of the direction for our lives needs to come from the following question: **What do I want?**

We can't wait for life to just happen to us. We can't allow pre-programming from our infancy to be the determining force for our future. We can't let well-meaning, or not so well-meaning, people in our present/past lives have such a huge say in what and how our lives should unfold each day.

We need to accept the responsibility that we are "in charge" of our lives. If we are living in ways that are not to our liking, then we have to do something about it.

What do I want? And what am I prepared to do to get what I want?

Decide what you want, how you want your life to be—
or someone else will decide for you.

WATCH YOUR LANGUAGE

Say what you want, not what you don't want.

There is a great deal of power in words. Do words plant a seed in our minds and, believing this to be true, we then make it happen? The mind is a very powerful force and we don't want it being directed by words that create negative thoughts or feelings. Instead, we want to speak positively, look for the good in people and events, and thereby influence the amount of positive in our lives.

What I hear very often from my clients is what I call **others language**, i.e., language that indicates they should be doing more for, others. Their mission in life is to take care of others. The language that they have been taught by their family of origin, community, culture, and/or church is "others" language. Do for others, but for self? I teach people to think about and use **self-language**, self-love language, the language of health, self-care, and the consistent pursuit of the question, "What do I want?"

Despite the current emphasis on wellness and self-care, it seems that for some people it is quite impossible for them to think about themselves, even when they are encouraged to do so. Paraphrasing Hans Selye, the reason you take good care of yourself is so you can reinvest your energy back into people. It makes good sense to learn self-language, but as we are aware, in this hard-driving world, logic and sense do not always win out. It is **positive language** that needs to be consistently repeated if there is to be any hope for change to occur.

We need to consciously use language that will reflect decisionour to be healthier, to repeat healthy sayings and affirmations until our mind accepts this as the truth and we begin to take better care of ourselves. Conversely, when we are better taken care of, we take better care of those around us. Remember, the mind doesn't differentiate between should and shouldn't, good and bad—it only hears the directive. Be sure the directive you are giving your mind is consistent with your health and well-being goals. Watch your language, say what you want for yourself, and say it often.

Take care of self first, then others.

WHAT DO I WANT?

As people proceed through life stages, I often hear them ask the question, "**Who am I?**" They feel they need to take time out to examine and explore this question, often in mid-life with unhappy consequences.

Perhaps the question that bears repeating is: "**What do I want?**"

"Who am I?" changes with living. It is a place in life determined by status and experience. It is not an "existential life position" determined by inner qualities and personality traits. "Who am I?" cannot be nailed down or defined, and is much too elusive to be a goal or purpose. However, it is a good question to ask if we merely want to talk, intellectualize, and "do nothing."

"What do I want?" requires specific and observable behaviors. The answer to this question requires us to clarify our thoughts and feelings, to be concise and realistic, and to think in "do-able" behaviors.

You can ask, "Who am I?" or "Who have I been in the past?" but the real question is, "What do I want?" now and in the future.

My power is in stating what I think, feel, value, and believe.
My power is not in getting others to fulfill my expectations.

WHO AM I?

When counseling or doing therapy, it is not usually a good idea to make a habit of giving clients the answers to their own questions. You are supposed to help them find the answers for themselves. On top of that, when the question is along the lines of "What is the 'meaning of life'," it is not advisable to set yourself up by answering it.

Be that as it may, there I was being asked the elusive philosophical question, "So, how do you know **who you are**?" Without the slightest hesitation, my mouth responded before my brain kicked into gear. I was not aware that I knew the answer to this question, but there I was answering it. My client, a woman in crisis and at a crossroads in her life, had a dilemma. Does she remain that which has been defining her—mother, wife, daughter, community club worker—or is there more to her? She felt she had lost herself in her desire to please others and make life comfortable for those she loved. "But who am I?" she painfully asked again. "I have lost who I am. I don't know where my roles end and I begin."

"Perhaps," I said without consciously thinking, "you are what you think, feel, value, and believe." My simplistic answer was out and exposed, looking quite frail and undernourished. But she nodded, smiled and said, "You're right. I need to start expressing what I think and feel and value and believe more often." I nodded in feeble agreement.

My foray into one of the greatest philosophical mysteries of life had been rewarded, I had expressed myself, and I was still alive and functioning. This realization gave me a jump in my step for the rest of the day.

For another perspective on the question of Who Am I? See *What Do I Want?* page 61.

Who are you?
You are what you think, feel, value, and believe.

DRAMA TRIANGLE

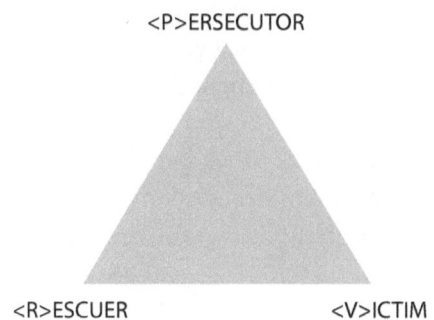

*Roles people play to help them through life
without having to be authentic.*

In the drama triangle, **the rescuer** (<R>) takes responsibility for people because they genuinely believe they know better. In turn, they get much-needed strokes—units of recognition—for taking care of others. This is traditionally a female role, although not exclusively so. **The victim** (<V>) has been trained or comes to believe that they can't take responsibility and need someone to show him/her how. This is the most powerful position on the triangle. Power and control is the way the <V> get their strokes.

The persecutor (<P>) is a role that is played as a response when either the <R> or <V> decides to stop playing their games. The <P> often uses guilt to get the <R> and <V> back where they "should" be.

<R> turned <P> says, "After all I have done for you!" when the <V> chooses to stop being dependent.

<V> turned <P> says, "I can't, and if you really cared and were really a good person, you would help me!" And so the roles continue with no effective end in sight.

All these roles are interchangeable in that one person can play all three roles at different times with different people. We generally find, however, that there is a pattern and that a person has a favorite or most often called-upon role. Most importantly, when we are on the **drama triangle**, the communication is not direct and, since nothing is really resolved, it goes nowhere. The unhealthy needs of the role players are met at the expense of the other person(s), which is totally dysfunctional.

The <R> takes on the responsibility of saving others for two unhealthy reasons:

- their own needs are met, and
- they feel they are in control, i.e., in the Top Dog position. The <R> gets their strokes at the expense of the <V>.

The helper however, assists other people to get their needs met. (See *Responsible vs. Helpful*, page 65.) Recognizing when you are communicating from one of the dysfunctional roles on the drama triangle will help you to make choices:

- to continue to be an <R> and get your needs met,
- to continue to be a <V> and feign powerlessness while controlling,
- to be a <P> and guilt people back to their familiar but dysfunctional role, or
- to get off the Drama Triangle and "get a life" through quality of life activities and being in balance. Then stroke self for doing these activities/behaviors.

*By being authentic and "getting a life,"
we solve a great many problems.*

<R>escuers rescue to get their own needs met—and help create victims.
Helpers help so that others get their needs met—and do good.

RESPONSIBLE VS. HELPFUL

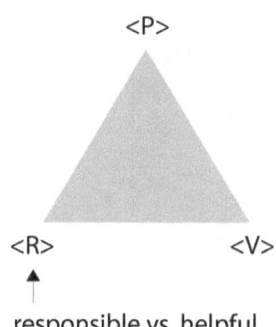

responsible vs. helpful

taking <R>esponsibility for <V>ictims vs. being helpful to people

I ask people the question, "Would you rather be responsible for people or helpful to them?" The answer always is *helpful*.

Yet, that's not what I see them do in their daily lives. Many people are programmed by their family of origin, culture, and community to be so helpful that they end up taking responsibility for others. Remember the golden rule: **never do for others what they can do for themselves**.

Taking responsibility for others is often seen as a good thing; not only by the person doing the rescuing, but also by the system the person works and lives in. Yes, systems do support the idea that the responsible person should stay that way and ought not to change.

The "r" in "responsibility" really stands for *rescuing*. And we know where that leads—nowhere. Just more drama! If you want things to be different, to be genuinely helpful, then you must help the individual move off the Drama Triangle (see page 63). Only then can they start developing options for their own issues without outside intervention. Remember, **Helpers** help people sort out options to their problems, but usually don't include themselves as one of the options.

Rescuers (<R>) set it up so they are the only option.

The <R> gets their stroke needs met by rescuing. The helper gets their stroke needs met by seeing other people get their needs met.

To lessen the stress load in your life, you need to encourage people to discover their own options for their own lives. Make it clear that in most situations, you are not one of the options.

Earn strokes through "having a life," not through rescuing.

*When you spend your life rescuing, you don't have a life—
you have a bunch of service contracts.*

*Definition of insanity: doing the same thing over
and over and expecting a different outcome.*

STOP COLLECTING OTHER PEOPLE'S MONKEYS

Let's take rescuing one step further so you can "see" how rescuing affects the rescuer.

Imagine people's problems looking like a monkey poised on their shoulder and the bigger the problem, the bigger the monkey. They come in just to talk to you, but somehow in the course of the conversation, their monkey magically slips over from their shoulder to yours. Maybe it was when you said, "How can I help?" or "Leave it with me" or/and "I will see what I can do!"

Even though it is just a small monkey, the problem is that another person will come by and leave their monkey, then another. You see how **collecting monkeys**—rescuing—isn't generally an isolated behavior. It becomes a lifestyle or a management style.

So you now have the responsibility for another person's monkey, and you know, in two or three days, that person will drop by just to see how you are making out with their monkey. Hmm, what a set up! No wonder rescuers—monkey collectors—often get so irritable, frustrated and resentful. They are tired of carrying other people's monkeys and then getting heck for not solving their problems sooner.

Stop collecting other people's monkeys and let them figure out what it is they need to do to solve their own problems. The next time somebody stops by your office or classroom (or at a staff meeting) with a monkey on their shoulder, make sure they take it with them when they leave. Spend time with them, but make sure your doing so is for the purpose of exploring options with them, not taking responsibility for them and their problems.

There is an old saying: "You should always go home with the person who brought you." In reference to monkeys: "They should always leave with the person who brought them."

"NICE" AND "PLEASING" JUST DON'T WORK

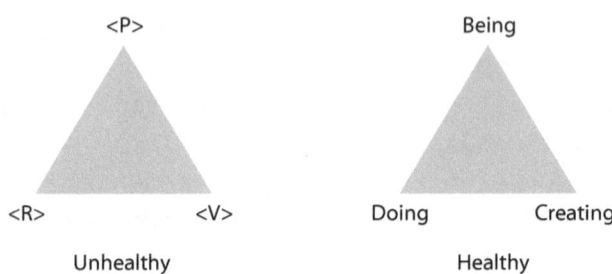

I have explained the drama triangle's <R>, <V> and <P> roles to clients and groups hundreds of times, but just recently I learned something new about this concept (see *Drama Triangle*, page 63).

There are **healthy strokes** one gets for:

- *Being:* a good nurse, a good person, a good friend
- *Doing:* going to work, coaching, building a fence
- *Creating:* joy, fun, beauty

There are also **unhealthy strokes**, which are the ones you get when you rescue people.

Many people in their very early lives learned to survive by exhibiting "nice," "pleasing," and "rescuing" behaviors. That was very acceptable in their families and was the result of adults teaching kids to be "good" and "nice" as a way of surviving in the world and being in that family.

I am not saying all people had to learn to be "nice" to survive their family of origin, but many did and went on to a life of niceness, pleasing, and rescuing. That is how many people got the strokes they needed to survive—being nice and helpful to people.

Everybody needs a quota of strokes daily to be healthy, so they learned that having people depend on them to do things for them was a consistent way to get their stroke quota filled. You might ask how can something that feels so good be so unhealthy and dysfunctional?

Simply put, rescuers (<R>) rescue to get their stroke needs filled. Helpers help other people to get their needs met. Rescuing is self-serving in that it is not helpful to others; rather, it is using others. Besides, if you rescue, you must have a victim (<V>). The training and maintenance of being a victim is not what helping people is about. (See *The Law of Diminishing Returns*, page 97.)

To break this dysfunctional cycle of getting strokes through rescuing, you need to focus on other ways to fill your stroke quota. The more important of these is paying attention to your own health and enjoying life. In other words, start to give strokes to yourself for taking care of yourself, and stop stroking yourself for overworking and rescuing others.

Starting to take better care of self instead of other people can be extremely difficult. Perhaps there is a balance where you get some strokes for being genuinely helpful to others, and some from being genuinely helpful to yourself. (See *Work vs. Health Messages*, page 32.)

Life is about making choices.

The absolute in "personal power" is the expression of our thoughts, feelings, values, and beliefs. We cannot change anyone, but we can state who we are (T F V B). People change themselves if they so choose.

TO BE AN 8...CONGRUENCY AND SELF-LOVE ARE THE KEY, NOT A RELATIONSHIP

*Relationships don't get us to an 8 on a 10-point scale—
being congruent and loving oneself does.*

A client and I were discussing how far he had come in the past year since his wife left him. In the beginning, there were days when he believed he couldn't make it without the relationship. I asked him, on a 10-point scale, where he was now compared to a year ago. He was now an "8"—so much change in one year!

I stated, "Imagine you're feeling like an "8" and you're not in a relationship. What allows you to feel so good?"

"Doing stuff I want to do, saying what I want instead of what I should," he responded.

People look to their relationship as the source of their "feeling good." Perhaps it's the line of work I am in and having to deal with so many relationships breaking up, but I see many relationships diminishing people's satisfaction with their life. Couples expect their relationship to enhance their life and are terribly disappointed when the relationship sours and takes away from the joy in their lives.

If you look to a relationship to make your life an "8," it is like building a house on quicksand. I believe you ought not to give the responsibility for your life being fulfilled and satisfying to anyone but yourself.

Don't trade in a healthy, self-sufficient "8" life for the hollow adulation and a few "crummy strokes" from the not-right person. Certainly invite another person into your life but don't put them in charge of your "8"-ness. If they add to your "8," they stay! If they subtract from your "8," they go! Easy to say but not to do!

Where this practical approach to relationships falls apart is in the fact that people are not always rational and reasonable. They have feelings that cloud their judgment, and lead them into and keep them in unhealthy relationships.

Being congruent and loving oneself gets us to an "8."

8s really challenge "red flags" in relationships.

*Being an 8 without someone
is better than being a 4 with someone.*

*Be sure your relationship enhances your
life—not takes away from it!*

THIRD FAMILY

We cannot form new relationships and make them work by using the same dysfunctional behaviors learned in our **family of origin**.

Yes, we did learn to survive rather well in that family using certain behaviors and methods of communication. Introducing a new person into our life with their own set of functional and dysfunctional behaviors, and expecting the relationship to work without compromise and change, is simply too much to ask. You can't continue to use original family behaviors in your **new family**.

Instead, you need to create a **third family** approach. You bring one set of behaviors that might not have worked all that well in your family of origin, and your partner brings a second fallible set. You automatically assume you can simply overlay these methods of communication and that the daily business of living will just work out. However, what actually happens is that the stronger of the two will dominate. Getting your own way is not free, and there is often a great deal of resentment and retaliation.

People from totally different family systems cannot expect that what worked in each family of origin will work in this new family, if indeed it worked the first time. We need to understand that change and compromise are required to allow this new "third family" to evolve. We need to be open to how our partner "sees the world" and, in turn, we need to be heard. From this openness comes new ways of providing for and meeting both our partners and our own needs and wants.

Couples need to work harder at creating new behaviors, different communication patterns, and **new rules** for the third family, instead of forcing their partner to accept their old ways of "seeing the world" as the "only way."

The sharing of "my truth" is intended to help my partners. Dumping on them is hurtful.

BACKYARD

I have often drawn simple, overlapping squares when working with couples to illustrate either:

- that some successful couples do not need a lot of time doing positive activities together to have a strong relationship; or
- that despite couples' individuality and lifestyle choices, they can have a strong relationship as long as there is agreement on some activities, "really important" activities (depending on their values—family gatherings, anniversaries, religious holidays), and that they be done together in harmony.

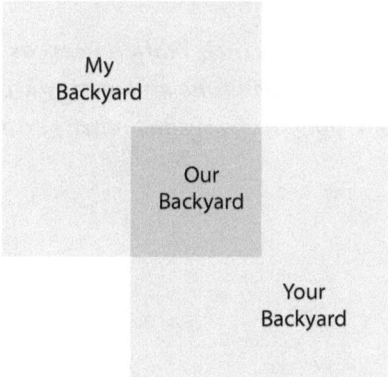

I've met couples whose backyards totally overlap, in other words, were "marriages made in heaven" but ultimately failed. I've seen backyards with a small "our," and yet the relationship was strong. People in relationships are different and therefore need a variety of activities and strokes to feel fulfilled. Just because somebody says "I do" doesn't mean they inherited an obligation to fulfill all their partner's needs.

Most of us need "variety" and "spice" (Hans Selye) to feel fulfilled. Often, one person has an expectation that the other should meet their needs. This is okay for a while, but eventually the partner feels smothered by that expectation, ends up being resentful, and begins to pull away.

In partnerships, there is a definite advantage in seeing "differences are strengths" as a truism. For many, their paradigm might have to be changed to make the statement work. Individual partners need to understand they are responsible for getting their own needs met—it is not their partner's responsibility. It needs to be realized that expecting partners to be all things and to be there for the other all the time is unworkable, unhealthy, and leads to dependency.

Someone choosing to go to the ballet or golfing and not including their partner is not symptomatic of growing apart, but merely needing different stimulation to be healthy. Some successful partnerships have very small backyards, while others are extensive and overlapping. Both are considered normal and healthy.

Taking a "time out" is considered "relationship protection."

Individuals need different activities and experiences to feel fulfilled.

*Partners need to see their "differences" as strengths,
otherwise too much time and energy are wasted
on trying to change the other person.*

NUMBER ONE (#1)

*"Make them feel like they are number one in your life.
Then you'll have the cooperation you need to take care of yourself."*
Dan Rosin

If I'm to take care of me, to set aside time for physical and recreational activities, to have social time with my friends, self-improvement and financial lectures, and be involved in therapeutic activities like woodworking or music, then I had better figure out first how to make my significant other feel like she is #1 in my life.

I know this is not true for all relationships, but think about it. If I figure out what my significant other needs and help her to get those needs met—and work at it consistently—is it not more likely that we would have a stronger relationship? That there would be greater understanding and more flexibility when it comes to those things of which she is not a part of in my life?

The formula is simple. "I treat you like you are the most important person in my life—which you are—and you understand and are ok with those things that only I like to do"—i.e., golfing. This appears to be quite simple, quite logical but people live in their emotions. This lesson has greater implications than just for couples. The world might be more cooperative if we convinced nations that they were important to us, that we are willing to do anything for them, did it, and then did it consistently. They'd know we cared and then they would be open to do the same for us. Yes? Treat people in caring ways and they will reciprocate and care about you. Is this too simple, too naive? Am I missing something?

*Treat people as if they were #1 in your life and soon
you will become #1 in theirs.*

DUPLICATION

I've worked with people who show particular symptoms—fear of rejection, being a "people pleaser," having low self-esteem.

I introduce these people to the concept of **duplication**, which means, "What I do, you will do," to help them look at their world differently. The concept is especially useful with couples, although it is applicable to just about every type of relationship. Let me explain.

If one person in the relationship is courteous, it's reasonable to assume courtesy will be returned; if one is kind, there's an excellent chance that the other will respond with kindness; if one is loyal, one's partner will more likely reciprocate. When one person models positive behavior, there is a good chance the partner will duplicate it.

Duplication is a different way of asking one's partner to reciprocate with similar positive behaviors. "When I treat you well, I expect that you will treat me well. I will start and hope you will **duplicate** my lead. I know you know what to do, I just hope you will do it."

Reasonable? Indeed! However, this doesn't always work, partners must have the right attitude.

The gap between knowing and doing may be the most formidable bridge you will ever have to cross.

GAP

The gap in a spark plug can't be too wide or the electrical impulse won't be able to jump across the space and start the car. If the gap between teeth is just right, it can be interpreted as alluringly beautiful, but if it is too wide, it becomes unsightly and isn't considered attractive. I believe there is a **gap principle** in relationships, too.

After the wedding and honeymoon are over, passions sometimes cool, and the reality of who each partner is becomes clearer. Any differences between the partners can serve to create a gap, and although this can be a natural spacing, the relationship needs to be worked on if the spark is going to continue to jump between the two individuals. Just like a spark plug.

What is "in common" becomes neutral, but the differences often get magnified. Differences can be strengths if there is maturity and an appreciation of each other, an acceptance of how we are different. All too often, however, these differences lead to a progressive widening of the gap.

Some of the differences I have noticed that can lend to a widening of the gap include: neat—messy; night owl—early riser; frugal—spender; intimate—cold; obsessed—balanced; motivated—laid back; happy—depressed.

Partners don't have to be the same, but they do have to realize that if the gap gets too wide, the relationship will strain, stretch, snap and separate. You can have different approaches and foci, be as different as day and night, and the relationship can still be healthy. However, you have to communicate and acknowledge your differences. You can see these genuine **differences as strengths** rather than "You are doing this behavior to annoy me." "No, I am not. I am exhibiting this behavior because I am different from you."

The key to lessening the gap between people is open communication and demonstrating genuine **respect** for individual differences and strengths.

COULD HAVE BEEN

In my work with couples who are separating or divorcing, I see much sadness, personal recriminations, and guilt attached to the break-up. Generally, one of the partners wants to stay and work it out, while the other wants out of the relationship. Even if they stay for the sake of the kids, for financial reasons, or because of their fear of the unknown, there is much pain.

If there is a split, the first step is the **letting go** phase. To assist in this, I encourage the individual(s) to write about their experience in the relationship in a journal or a "progressive letter" to their partner. I ask them to recall three major things: the **good times**, the **not-so-good times**—why they find it difficult to stay together—and, by far the toughest to let go of, what **could have been**.

The "could have been" is that part of the relationship they have yet to live through—the future. The plans they talked about, the places they wanted to go, the children they aren't going to have, the retirement that won't be. No matter how unsatisfactory the relationship was, it is still difficult to let go of what "could have been"? Although to write about it is difficult, it probably is the most therapeutic thing partners can do for self as they separate.

If you have something or someone you need to let go of, include in your writing what was good, not so good, and what could have been. Write until you intuitively know you are done, and then stop.

Letting go is a process, not a decision.

YOU CAN'T FIX IT WHERE IT GOT BROKEN

If most disagreements that occur with your significant other seem to be occurring in the kitchen or bedroom, it becomes very difficult to work on solutions in those same places. Find a **neutral site**, where it is not one or the other's "territory." Public places like parks, restaurants and malls are good for discussions, as it is akin to having a third party present.

No matter what the level of intensity of your communication, if you determine a favorite place where you have been successful at handling these issues in the past, where you have a positive association, then chances are better that this place will result in a successful conclusion to your discussion. Certainly, a neutral place is better than remaining at home where the cues have quite often become negative or territorial.

I am not looking for the right answers, but merely a different position from which to view my options.

The "spark between people is easy to light, but not so easy to keep lit.

BUFFER TIME

In the morning, many people simply get up, get ready, and go to work—"have-to" activities. However, if we make time to go for a walk soon after we get up, then take a nice relaxing shower, enjoy a leisurely breakfast, and read the paper before heading to work, we are taking full advantage of **buffer time** which is the time in-between the "have-to" activities!

We may have a series of intense meetings, but between each we go to the staff room and chat with people, take a short walk, or talk on the phone with a special friend. This is buffer time, that time between activities when we relax and do things we really enjoy doing and don't have to do.

It's an appealing notion that we could have nothing but buffer time, with a few "have-to" activities thrown in. That may be dreaming, although it might be possible after retirement. Until that day when we have exclusive control over our time, we would do well to take care of the present by building in short, pleasant breaks that provide respite from intensive living.

*Golden time: that time we take for ourselves
when we are too busy to take it.*

WORRY VS. CONCERN

Worrying is a non-active, non-productive circuitous activity. The worry tape goes nowhere, nothing gets done, nothing changes, our body gets weakened, and our energy is depleted.

Concern, on the other hand, is positively driven and insists on action. Concern is an attitude that leads to action. And if it doesn't lead to action, perhaps it is not within our power to change the issue. We then need to "let go" of whatever concerns us.

Worry ⟶ Depleted energy

Concern ⟶ Action plan

Identify three worries that have been plaguing you recently
_____
_____
_____

Convert these worries to concerns.
I am concerned about:
_____
_____
_____

Develop a plan of action (if applicable).
My "Plan of Action" for each is:
_____
_____
_____

SPEED BUMP

Life is full of speed bumps, those annoying mounds of tar or concrete in shopping mall parking lots that prevent us from going too fast or, in an analogical sense, from enjoying life too much.

This speed bump analogy just popped out one day in a session with a client. He seemed to have a number of annoying individuals in his life with whom he had to deal and events he had to get through before things got easier. His life had many speed bumps.

Life is like that! We have to learn to work through the hassles and events, and sometimes we have to even ask people to leave, to move out of our lives before things can get better.

We can run at top speed at obstacles/problems/life, but, as with speed bumps, we might break a shock absorber, or worse yet, an ankle, an ego. Conversely, we can slow down, take it easy and enjoy the ride, even the bumps of life. If we go slow enough and enjoy the trip, there might not be any jarring at all.

We need to approach some of the speed bumps in our lives a little slower with the intention of taking really good care of our personal vessel. The thing about a speed bump is we can worry about it, do everything we can to avoid it—please and placate—or we can just go over it, be done with it, and move on in our lives.

If nothing can be done and the issue is beyond your power, accept it, let go, and move on!

I USED TO...

It seems to me that as people get more distressed, they talk more about what they **used to do**. I believe there is a relationship between their level of distress and how they talk about things they used to do. "I used to walk, play sports, we used to have dinner parties, go to theatre…but somehow all that has stopped." *I used to…*is not only a symptom of unbalance—too much work and/or not enough play—but also a major contributor to the individual's distress.

The good news is that it is not difficult to once again choose some of those activities, events and people of which and of whom you speak fondly when you say *I used to…*. Remember, you don't have to reinvent the wheel, but you do need to look at some of the things you **used to do** and just **do them more often**. This might be enough to get you back on track. What do you think?

Stop talking about what could be or should be and just loosen up and "do" life.

UNIVERSAL TRUTH – YOURS OR MINE?

I appreciate your truth; I also appreciate mine.
I respect your truth; I also respect mine.

Why is it we think we always have the right answer, or the correct way of dealing with a sticky problem? I remember a saying from my childhood, "Who died and made you King?," which means how do you figure you are right and the rest of us are wrong? Where did this idea come from that for me to be correct, you have to be wrong, or vice versa? Let's stop for a minute and ask our self, "Has divine intervention given me insight to see the world better than you? Just because I consider myself a generous, concerned, benevolent, caring human being, does that mean my perceptions are better than yours?"

We spend inordinate amounts of communication time trying to convince people that the way we see the world is the correct way, and they can only benefit from accepting that simple and true fact. Such a dogmatic perception of the truth often leads to power struggles, conflict and miscommunication.

Well, guess what? Others have the same feeling about the truth that we do. They believe earnestly that their perception is the correct one. Like us, they feel a responsibility, an obligation, and the right to see that we are straightened out, for our own good of course.

Power, force, bullying, intimidation, discounting, devaluing and put-downs are employed to get one's point of truth across. Of course, none of these methods, which are intended to change your position or view of the world, really work because you are also employing the same methods. You are trying to get me to understand and accept your view as the correct one. In fact, there is not much listening to or understanding of what either is saying, and we resort to jousting to determine who wears the crown.

When we both believe that we have the one and only correct view or set of facts, there are two options to consider: we can remain determined to share our truth with others, whether they ask for it or not, or we can stop and listen to their thoughts, feelings, values and beliefs (T F V B). We can **listen** and **not judge**.

When we start to listen, we may start to understand. Meanwhile, it is essential that we **understand** that our own truth, our T F V B, is valid. However, no one has **universal truth**, only his or her own truth. The goal here is to share "who" you are, but not to dump on those who hold a different view.

Perhaps if I listen to your truth, you might listen to mine.
At least we'd have a start to understanding each other!

Universal Truth...nobody has it!
We only have our own truth—and that is something to be proud of as long as we don't try to sell it as The truth.

YOU'RE NOT IT...

How did you get to be "It"? To have that feeling that you are responsible for all outcomes? When did you take over from God?

When did you put yourself on a mission and assume total responsibility for how circumstances turn out in your life and the lives of others? Well, I've got news for you, you are obsessed!

A client of mine, totally burned out, fried, was angry at having done everything for everybody with no one appreciating him or his efforts. He stated over and over that the system had failed him. It forced him to work long hours, take on extra projects, only to see others rewarded. To him, the others did not do their share, but knew how to manipulate and get what they wanted from the system. He wanted to kill them!

I wanted to tell him to stop blaming the system and to look after himself, to give up this mission, which was to make the system work, despite the personal cost. I felt compelled to tell him, "Only God could control and make better the system you work in, and you are not He/She/**It**."

When we become "It" in our own minds, we take responsibility for people and systems as if we had divine authority to do so.

When you think you're "It," your mission becomes to solve, to change, to cure…others. Consequently, you become at-risk emotionally and overly involved mentally. You are unbalanced and exhibit "crazy" behavior.

When you become "It," you take responsibility as if you were God. God can handle this responsibility, humans can't. You will get sick!

When you are 'It', you are of no value to anybody.
Yo u become obsessed, blind only to your mission.
You stop seeing what you're doing to yourself.
You lose perspective, you lose your health.

You: see "It"
      think "It"
      feel "It," and soon you
      become "It"…
…and shortly after, you become sick.

Healthy Caring: You state what you think, feel, value and believe.
You don't take responsibility for change outside of yourself.
You do what you can to be heard, and then you go home to your Real Life.

POWERLESSNESS Á FRUSTRATION Á ANGER

I do not have universal truth, just my own view—truth—of the world. That view has me believing that when I respond to a situation with anger, it's often because I feel somewhat powerless to change that situation. At those times, I do not feel in charge of my life.

Feeling of Powerlessness (leads to) → Feeling of Frustration → Anger

"If you—partner—don't love me anymore, or you—teen—stay out past your curfew, or I have to deal with you—difficult person—then I feel powerless because I can't change your behavior."

When a car cuts me off in traffic, my frustration and anger is centered on that act. I vow and act accordingly—"Nobody else is going to push me around." My over-reaction to this situation is often the result of feeling frustrated and powerless by some other events in my life.

We need to be clear on what we can change and what we cannot, to accept the fact that we are powerless to change others. We need to understand that the only real power we have is to state our T F V B. People change themselves. They make decisions themselves. Our words may influence them to the extent that they think or conclude something, but it is their process that leads them to their conclusions.

We can decrease the number of anger episodes in our lives if we stop expecting people to be like us, and learn to state our T F V B only as "our" truth, not "the" truth.

Lowering your expectations lowers your frustration, lowers the number of anger episodes.

ANGER BEGETS ANGER

One does not learn to control one's anger unless motivated to do so!

I do not yell at my wife or children because I want them to respect me and to feel safe. Unfortunately, many people do not support this value. Aware of the violence in the world today, for example "road rage," I don't yell and make gestures at a person cutting in and out of traffic because he may be unstable and harm me. I don't get angry with my boss—at least to his face—because he may fire me.

Controlling anger is often about **discipline**, about knowing what is appropriate and then doing it. Dumping my anger on others may temporarily get what I want, but am I willing to pay the price of loss of respect, love and security from those I yell at?

Anger needs to be "worked out" with people rather than "dumped on" them. By "working out," I mean talking about your anger instead of physically being angry. Use "I" language and keep interactions short. *Talk about and talk out your anger.* Don't just let it "all hang out" because you feel justifiably upset.

Being angry only promotes more anger.
"Talk about," don't "be" angry.

Anyone can become angry—that is easy.
But to be angry with the right person, to the right degree,
at the right time, for the right purpose,
in the right way—that is not easy.

STROKES AND CONSCIENTIOUS OBJECTORS

I read a few articles about starvation studies that were conducted on a group of Conscientious Objectors (COs), people who chose not to fight in WWII. My understanding is that our government incarcerated these people, and in lieu of further punishment, they volunteered to be part of experiments dealing with the effects of starvation.

It seems that the digestive system of COs became so finely tuned due to their starvation conditions, that they could virtually get nourishment from a mossy stone. Their bodies became so adept at utilizing whatever nourishment was available that they learned to survive on very little food, and yet remained remarkably healthy.

Presently, it seems to me that the human condition is such that people are metaphorically "starving" because they lack strokes (units of recognition). Humans need a certain number of strokes daily to be healthy, but are falling far short of the necessary quota. I contend that we should learn to get more stroke-value out of the people, jobs and lifestyles we are presently in, rather than continually looking for more/better/different. Like the COs, we need to learn to be healthier by fully utilizing each stroke given to us. Only now am I beginning to fully understand this principle, and how it allows me to get more from what I actually have in my life instead of wishing for more, or changing jobs, people or locations, with the hope of feeling better/receiving more strokes.

I tell the following to my lonely and hurting clients who are surrounded by people but not able to seek nourishment from them: "You may need 50 strokes a day to be healthy, so don't fire even the least important people in your life. Don't get rid of the 2-stroke or 3-stroke people just because they are not the 30-stroke love of your life, or because they don't consistently do what you want or expect. Take what they give you. Be able to get a stroke from a stone. You may need ten 5-strokers to be healthy because you don't have a 30-stroke significant other, or because your significant other has lost stroke status in your life. To be healthy, you must accept that the onus is on you to acquire the strokes you need—from all available sources."

Rather than look elsewhere, we need to make a commitment to what we have, the people who are already in our lives, to stroke them more and learn how to get more strokes from them. There is a great deal of nourishment (strokes) right where we are, and it can be obtained from the many people in our present lives. We need to fine tune our stroke receptors to allow ourselves to get more from the existing people —partners, staff, friends— rather than thinking we will get more by changing them as well as our jobs, geography, apartments, cars, and stereo equipment.

You will get more when you give more.

Reverse the pattern: learn to give yourself strokes for doing good work after good play.

PLEASING AND PLACATING – EARLY "HOW TO MAKE IT" MESSAGES

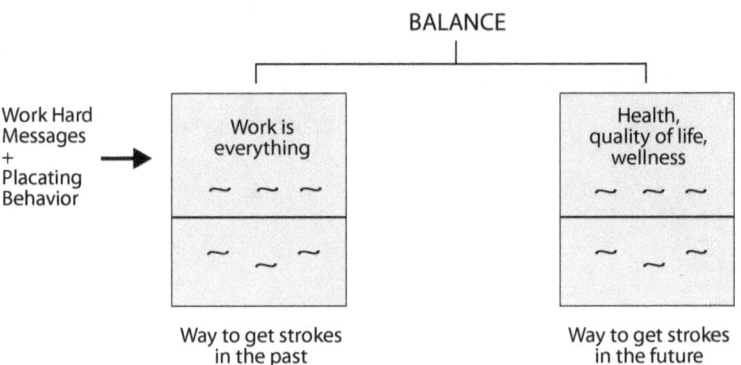

In addition to the multitude of work-hard messages on the computer "chip" in our brains, our parents taught us how to "make it" by developing pleasing and placating personalities:

- Think about others, not yourself
- Be passive rather than assertive
- Don't make waves
- Be helpful

In the past, we learned to get our strokes from two major sources: working hard at our jobs, and being accepted as a nice, pleasing and placating person.

I believe it is time to rethink how we want to get our strokes in the present and future. Instead of being nice, let's consider making good decisions around health issues—having more fun, relaxing more often and, in general, improving the quality of our lives. **Wellness, health, and quality of life** are the criteria we would now use when deciding what strokes to value. It means changing the criteria for what gets stroked. For example, quality of life and health-related activities would receive the highest value of strokes. Overwork and pleasing- type behavior would not be rewarded.

In the past, we overvalued work. The image we strove for was one of a pleasing, placating type of person, and in these ways we learned to get our quota of strokes. However, we can change! We can learn to value health, quality of life and wellness behaviors, and make them the new criteria upon which to establish our personal goals. We can learn to give ourselves strokes for making good health decisions and not just relying on work-related strokes.

Prior to realizing you were trained to be a pleaser/placator, didn't you ever get suspicious when everyone else was getting served and you weren't?

About work: know when to start, but even more important, know when to stop.

HEALTHY VS. UNHEALTHY STROKES

"We are never totally cured of our dysfunctional need to rescue, but we can learn to make conscious choices about our time and energy (boundaries) that will allow us to lead a better and more balanced lifestyle."
Dan Rosin

Quite simply, healthy strokes are those we get and give for legitimate reasons, for doing good stuff, for being a good person, for caring. One area of dysfunctional behavior in which we receive unhealthy strokes is rescuing people (see *Drama Triangle*, page 63). We learn early in life that there are stroke rewards for pleasing and being nice that eventually lead to rescuing behaviors. We grow up to be adults who are then dependent, almost exclusively on this one way of acquiring their strokes—through rescuing.

If we are to be healthy individuals, we must learn how to get our stroke quota met in ways other than rescuing (see *Strokes and Conscientious Objectors*, page 90, and *Responsible vs. Helpful*, page 65).

Perhaps understanding what healthy strokes are and giving more emphasis to these in your sphere of influence will net you more positive strokes, so that you will have less of a need to go for the rescuing variety.

The impulse to get a quick rescue fix never really leaves a person. However, if we learn to get our "pot" filled in healthy ways, we certainly will be less inclined to allow ourselves to be pulled back into rescue behavior. We will then create other methods of acquiring the strokes that we need to be healthy and in balance.

Balance—when networking overtakes overworking.

CHANGE THE FILTER FROM ACCOMPLISHMENT TO HEALTH

Workaholics often have the following message in their heads: "You are worthy only when you are accomplishing." This message is often received early in life, usually from their family of origin. I see this as a problem for many, because their options are restricted and they have to earn the majority of their strokes through work-related "accomplishments."

For most of my life, there has been an internal pressure to maintain this accomplishment pattern. Until recently, the only "accomplishments" that had meaning for me were those connected with work of some kind. I acknowledge that "work accomplishments" are valid and meaningful to our lives because they improve self-esteem and help us keep our jobs. However, they are not the only accomplishments for which we need to stroke ourselves.

Other accomplishments we may choose to stroke ourselves that would allow us to get more balance in our lives include: **health and well-being** choices, **quality of life** (QL) choices, and commitment to a **wellness lifestyle**. We may choose to see fun, relaxation and pleasurable activities as accomplishments worthy of strokes. We do have a choice!

What we need to establish is a balance between "work accomplishments" and "health-oriented accomplishments" to earn our strokes. We need to rethink just what is important to us and not always put work first. For many of us, we have been sacrificing our health and our balance so as to get the work done. Now it is time to give self more strokes for engaging in healthy, fun activities.

DIVERSIFY

When we are falling in love, we see our loved one as the most exciting and wonderful person in the world. For a period of time, we seem to feel that this one person can do it all for us, provide our entertainment, our laughter, closeness and strokes. Our friends who feel abandoned and claim that we no longer need them often criticize us during this period.

When we marry, there is the belief that the loved one is supposed to fulfill all our needs and provide all the strokes we will need to be healthy. Why else would we marry them? It seems true for a while, but when the honeymoon is over and we get down to a life that includes our career and our other roles in life—sibling, friend, parent—things change.

It seemed that when we were in the honeymoon stage of our life— pre-marriage and the first year or two of marriage—our job and the various activities and roles we played were what we did in between contact with our loved one. Eventually, our jobs, activities and life are put into a more realistic perspective, and we begin to realize these are important to us as well as the other person.

It is essential we understand that these other things—job, activities, and roles—are equally as important as our partner to make life fulfilling. If we don't realize this, we'll soon be starving for strokes, for no one person or activity can provide the stimulation and diverse experience to completely fill up our **stroke pot**. If we look to only one person, we will starve and become frustrated and resentful with that person.

Our need for strokes from a **variety of sources** is like a financial portfolio. For the portfolio to be healthy and perform well, it needs to be diversified. We need a variety of people and activities in our life to provide the strokes for us to be happy and healthy.

THE LAW OF DIMINISHING RETURNS

People from our early years—parents, grandparents, older siblings, community, culture, school—taught us how to get the strokes needed to be healthy. We learned that if we did "this" behavior, we would more than likely receive "these" kinds of strokes. What I see happening with many of my clients is that they have been rewarded with positive strokes for being a certain way. Consequently, they have developed behaviors so as to receive the complement of strokes they need for them to be healthy.

For example, if the person has always been helpful by putting other people first—friends, family, neighbors—and thereby seeing them get their needs met, you call them a good girl or boy. They get their strokes by **being good** or helpful or available. This is how they've always earned the majority of their strokes, and society definitely encourages this kind of behavior.

However, at some point in their adult life, they discover two things:

- the **Law of Diminishing Returns** is in effect. That is, they are doing as much as ever for people, maybe even more, and receiving half the strokes they used to get for the same service; and
- they don't feel "in charge" of their lives but rather controlled by people who want them to continue being "good." Their behavior is good for others, but not for themselves.

While working with a client and writing on a plastic sheet on the back of my office door, this diagram popped into my brain:

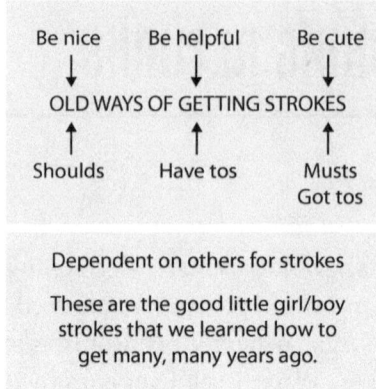 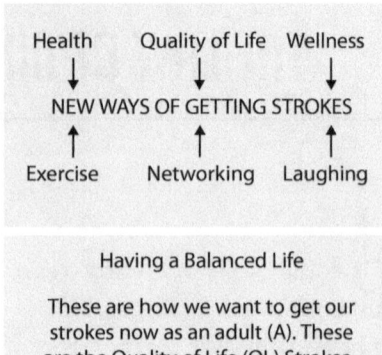

Take a moment to look at the reasons you have been getting Strokes—the old way.

Identify specific behaviors that you would say are the strokes that keep you being "good little girls/boys"—behaviors you still do today because you should or because somebody might get mad or be disappointed if you stopped doing them—e.g., if you stopped having lunch with a parent three times a week.

Look at how you get your strokes the old way, and identify specific behaviors.

OLD WAYS OF GETTING STROKES
_____
_____
_____
_____

Now decide how you want to get strokes in the here and now.
NEW WAYS OF GETTING STROKES
_____
_____
_____
_____

If you have gotten strokes all your life for rescuing and serving others, it is not easy to switch to giving yourself strokes for doing healthy, fun loving, quality of life, wellness-type activities. But, thankfully, many people are realizing that the anger and resentment they feel at being trapped in a lifestyle with a set of behaviors in which they take care of others but not themselves, is no longer acceptable and is motivating them to change.

To complete the learning, look at the benefits you got from the old system and the price of continuing that system. Then do the same for new ways of getting strokes.

OLD WAYS OF GETTING STROKES

Benefits	Price
_____	_____
_____	_____
_____	_____
_____	_____

NEW WAYS OF GETTING STROKES

Benefits	Price
_____	_____
_____	_____
_____	_____
_____	_____

Change has a price tag!
There is an internal price for keeping things the same,
and an external price when those around
you react to the changes.

CRUMMY STROKES

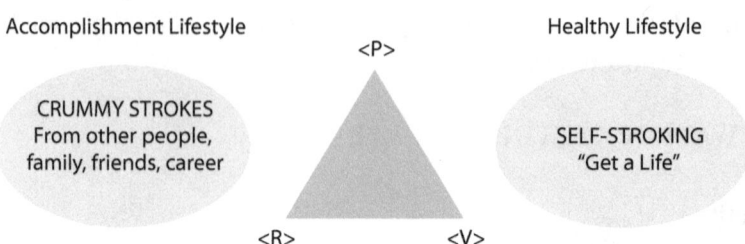

We can become so dependent on strokes from certain others that we are willing to settle for little and continue to starve, rather than take appropriate action. Others realize that we are needy and dependent on them, so they throw us crumbs from time to time, little bits of themselves when it is convenient for them. Hence, the name **Crummy Strokes**.

We need to stop being so dependent on other people, on our jobs, and on our clients/students for the strokes we need for us to stay healthy. We need to stroke ourselves more often for who we are and what we do. We need to change the criteria for strokes, from "how much did I accomplish," to "how many healthy and fun things did I do for myself today."

*When I adequately stroke myself,
I depend less on emotional crumbs from others.*

DEPENDENT ON OTHERS?

Roughly translated, a portion of the Gestalt Prayer says:

> *I have my life and you have yours*
> *If our paths cross that will be great*
> *If they do not cross, I will still have a great life*

I talk with many people who have become dependent on others or on addictive activities—e.g., overwork—to complete their lives, to provide the strokes they need to be healthy. It is ironic that these people expect to maintain their health from the strokes received through unhealthy behaviors—e.g., dependency, addictions.

What needs to be understood is that everything you need to have a great life exists solely within yourself. We may invite other people to enhance our lives, but "make" our lives? No!

Let us take responsibility for our own lives. If we have a good life, we should hug ourselves. If we have a bad life, we need to ask the question, "What can I do to make it better?" Not everything is in our power, but our response to everything is within our power.

> *I don't need you to have a great life.*
> *But I want you to enhance what I have started.*

80-20 RULE

Stroke your self!
What a novel concept.

Eighty percent of the strokes we need to be healthy ought to come from ourselves and 20% from others. However, due to society's teachings, most of us find it very difficult to stroke ourselves. We have been taught that to say or acknowledge good things about ourselves will lead to conceit, arrogance, and a swelled head. As a consequence, we have learned not to stroke ourselves, even when we are doing good things. Instead, we have come to depend on others to provide the strokes we need to be healthy. This practice puts us in a very tenuous position, with the result that we could potentially "starve" ourselves (see *Too High a Price*, page 103).

We need to do and be things we believe in and then stroke our self for doing and being them.

We need to give ourselves permission to focus on what we are doing, our positive life activities, and see this as our method of acquiring the strokes we need, rather than waiting for others to stroke us.

Give yourself lots of strokes for being you.
Others don't "make" your life; they "enhance" your life.
Love yourself first—and often.

TOO HIGH A PRICE

Loving yourself is enough! (See *80–20 Rule*, page 102.) If you have to depend on other people or a significant relationship for the majority of your strokes to feel OK, or to raise or maintain your self-esteem, then there is a danger that you may be paying too high a price.

When you give someone the power to make you feel good or important, you also give away the power to do that for yourself. For example, in education, giving power to a group of teenagers who are starving for strokes themselves, just to make *you* feel better is neither wise nor healthy. To feel good about yourself only when you are receiving strokes from the love interest in your life (dependency) instead of for who you are and what you are doing in all aspects of your life is equally dangerous. Also, being needy is not sexy, not attractive to the loved one. Giving away your personal power for short-term strokes is **too high a price**. We must learn to love ourselves, give ourselves strokes, and elevate our self-esteem.

Increasing your self-esteem is easy.
You simply do good things,
remember you did them and give
your self strokes accordingly.

JEALOUSY IS ABOUT LACK OF SELF-ESTEEM

*I love you so much that I just can't bear the thought of
you being with someone else.*

This statement isn't about love for another. It's about lack of love for oneself. What the person is actually saying is, "When I don't love myself, I focus on how "you love me." It never seems good enough. When my self-esteem is low, good feelings about myself don't come from me caring about me. Instead, these good feelings are only felt when you deem me loveable. Therefore, I am loveable only when you love me. Because I do that, I give you the power over how I feel about myself. So, when I feel jealous, it is really my fear that the strokes you give me by loving me might dry up. You might withhold them. So I get fearful and often angry, but rarely loving."

Jealousy, which has incorrectly been used as a standard to determine the depth of one's love, is not really love at all, but instead measures the degree of one's **lack of self-esteem**.

*Sometimes the upper level of our "success" is inversely
proportionate to the lowest level of our "self-esteem."*

WHY NOW?

"Why now?" is often asked by my clients who have survived some bad years, either in their personal or professional lives, without getting sick. So, why now, when things seem to be much better, are they getting sick, fatigued, and burned out?

When you are in a crisis, the head directs you to do what needs to be done. The body somehow finds the strength to execute the task. For example, situations that *(caregivers)* sometimes find themselves in include:

- a particularly tough client, with lack of support from their supervisor,
- people intent on hassling them and not caring a bit about their health,
- Prolonged stressful situations, as in dealing with sick/infirmed loved ones at home with little supports

No matter what the crisis, we seem to be able to handle it at the time. Sometimes it can be up to three years later when we fall apart and can't figure out why it has happened.

Chemicals released when we perceive danger—the old **Fight or Flight Syndrome**—can definitely carry us through some incredibly tough times and horrific crises. We rise to the occasion. The chemicals carry us through. Some people even become addicted to the "danger chemicals." After a time, the body thoroughly wears out. It's been putting out at a level much higher than normal, due to the influence of the chemicals sent by the brain, to allow us to do what we must. When the danger passes, we sometimes maintain the high level of activity for quite a while, but eventually we crash, and we come down a long way.

An example is a client who had recently received a few poor evaluations at work when previously in his career, he had received only excellent feedback. Disturbing physical symptoms included fatigue, loss of purpose, irritability, poor sleeping habits, loss of focus, poor memory, trouble buckling down to work and a feeling of losing control of his emotions. The overwhelming feeling was, "I don't want to be here anymore."

From where did this overpoweringly negative feeling come? Why the change from a gung-ho person, to one who was ready to abandon his chosen profession? We talked for a number of sessions and although I perceived the sessions to be helpful to him—being heard and listened to always feel good—there didn't seem to be any particular reason for this formerly competent person to suddenly feel and act incompetent.

However, a comment at the end of one session identified the root of the issue. Two years prior, he had a particularly difficult client whose spouse had promoted the difficulty. One day, the spouse came in to see my client, closed the door behind him, and throughout the ensuing conversation made several threatening remarks. The person felt intimidated, bullied and scared. He felt his life was over, but he never said anything about it. He rode it out, having to constantly overcome the many feelings that welled up every time he saw this client. Why didn't he report the incident to his superior? He had no idea, but whatever his reasons, they were certainly valid to him at the time. Can you imagine the high level of fear this situation produced? Indeed, the incredible amount of adrenaline and other "fight or flight" chemicals kept him in a permanent state of readiness to flee to protect him self if necessary.

Two years after this incident, with the client having moved on, this person found that they were unable to carry on effectively. "Why now?" he asked.

When evaluating the stress levels in our daily lives, it is important to understand that stress is cumulative. The experts have been saying for at least three decades that unresolved crisis or stress is stored in the muscle sheaths of our body. We need to understand that though the crisis is past, it is not over. For as long as three years after a crisis, we must be on guard for any changes in our physical and psychological health.

*Grief, trauma, change, despair—can't go around them,
have to go through them.*

AFTER THE BURNOUT...

When some of my clients are coming back from an illness or burnout, I often encourage them with the following words: "Stretch yourself. Do more than you have been doing, but not so much that you scare yourself or psychologically tear your self down."

Being off work due to illness has an effect on one's self-esteem. It's easier to return to the workplace if the illness has been a visible one— i.e., a broken leg, a bad back, an operation—but much more difficult if the illness has been due to a psychological issue brought about by stress.

Very often there is a real need to be away from the workplace and the usual working lifestyle for a certain amount of time to allow for the initial healing. But then there is a need to get back into the work situation—limited and protected at first—so as to confirm the healing and quickly attend to any self-esteem issues that have arisen by being away from the job. We are never truly ready to go back into the workplace.

It's like a theatre situation where the play is not ready to open but nonetheless opens anyway. Being off work does nothing to prepare us for going back, but at some point we just have to. Hopefully, the caregivers make it humane, slow and progressive, but we're never truly ready to return to the workplace that often invited us to get sick in the first place.

When you're off work due to illness (visible or otherwise), it's important to understand your need to return before being totally ready. Getting back to work is part of the recovery. Get into activities and get involved; however, don't do too much too soon.

Stretch—don't tear.

WORKPLACE TRAUMA AND A COMMITMENT TO HEALTH

I had been working with a severely stressed and burned-out social worker when the question of returning to work was broached. He was frightened at the prospect of returning to the "scene of the crime," the place that had so relentlessly invited him to get sick months before. We talked about the severity of burnout. When the mind perceives something a certain way, often the body follows its directions. This person was hard on himself, blaming his body, feeling it had let him down. He wanted to return to work "soon" because he felt guilt and shame at being off work. He wanted to end the feeling that he was taking advantage of the system and of his peers "still in the trenches." It was my opinion that healing still needed to take place before he could successfully re-enter the workplace, and I needed him to understand that.

It is clear to me that our bodies will not allow us to go back into a situation or workplace where it is perceived we have been traumatized, until we can assure the body that we know how to take care of it when we do return. We must be committed to and understand what taking care of our body means before we can return to work. Headaches, trembling, sleeplessness, no appetite and inability to focus are the body's way of telling us that it is not convinced we have significantly changed our lifestyle, that it is safe and we are on a positive track.

We need to convince the body that we will take care of it by practicing positive behaviors more often—by doing good things for it, by "having a life," by making good health decisions.

When we "walk the walk," our bodies can see that we are serious about health and not just "talking the talk." If our minds can see the evidence that we are serious and doing good things consistently for the body, then the mind—positive attitude—will work in conjunction with the body—caring behaviors—to produce improved health and, at some point, affect a more successful return to life and eventually the workplace.

PUSHING AND PUNISHING (PU + PU)

I realized I knew first-hand about Pu + Pu after dealing with a client who had much trauma and death in a short period of time in his life, compounded by an unwelcome job transfer. He felt very distressed, short-tempered, and had become very negative in his outlook. He referred to himself as Mr. "Half Empty," and compensated for his unhappy life by "pushing" himself at whatever he undertook.

This **pushing** was seen as **punishing** himself for the anger and resentment he felt at not being allowed in his family of origin to directly express his feelings to the appropriate people. He had been taught to maintain his image of "nice guy" at all costs. So, instead of confronting those who deserved those feelings, his negativity and anger leaked out onto his wife, kids, colleagues and friends. The final awareness came after his son's soccer game when he realized that he had once again yelled at the referee, the coach, and found fault with his son's performance. Ashamed and devastated that he was behaving in this manner, he dropped by my office and we talked.

He wanted not only to change his aggressive behavior, but also to get at what was causing him to have changed from being a "nice guy." The answer to "Why did I change?" became evident as he shared a lifetime of grief and resentment. What was most devastating was not that things happened to him; because he did realize that life throws people curveballs—problems—but rather that he had no permission to talk openly about his feelings. The message from his family of origin was clear—anger and upset was simply not allowed. He was to absorb all of the problems and subsequent feelings and remain stoic and, of course, a "nice guy."

"How would things be different if you were to become more congruent, if what came out of your mouth matched your thoughts and feelings?" This question started us in another direction that led to considering lifestyle changes and well- being as our goal. This man had rarely considered himself at all when making choices about how to spend his time and energy. After much introspective thinking, however, he began to realize that he did count and eventually his behavior changed to reflect that realization.

One of the exercises I gave him to help understand that he had a choice, was the dichotomy of an *either/or*. "You can either discipline yourself when you go to the soccer game, keep your mouth shut and focus on the fun the kids are having, or you can take your pushing, punishing behavior to greater extremes." When he felt anger at the game, he was to run as hard and as far away from the game as he could get in 10 minutes. He was to really push himself away, not allow this to leak out onto others, only himself. His eventual punishment was that he was tired from the run, and he had missed much of his son's game.

He now had a choice. He could decide which behavior made the most sense to him. He could **push** and **punish** himself, he could choose to **discipline** himself and say nothing, or he could be congruent with what was in his head.

If you are leaking—pushing and punishing: angry, irritable, finding fault—and people around you are paying the price, you might consider either acting like you aren't angry and resentful (discipline), or make the behavior overt and ten times as big. Hopefully, you will see the folly in this punishing behavior, and end up laughing or being disgusted with your self, and choose a different way to be. A third option, you can learn, is to be congruent with your thoughts and feelings, and deal directly and assertively with people.

You see? You do have a choice!

Talk − Action = 0
You don't get cured, you get better.

THE HALF EMPTY SYNDROME

Is this cup half empty or half full?
Am I running from something or to something?

I believe that: "Life is better when I focus on *what I do* have instead of what I don't."

"Life is better when I focus on *how much I have changed* instead of how far I have to go."

"It's not what you stop doing that is most important, but rather *what you start doing.*"

As I got healthier, I fancied myself as a more positive person. So it came as a very large shock one day when my daughter, Lisa, pointed out to me that I often used negative examples to scare people into thinking about wellness and making changes.

We were having breakfast at a local restaurant and I was trying an idea out on her I had for an article. The article was intended to inform wellness leaders in the school system that programs and slogans built on fear really didn't work in the long run—telling people that if they don't eat properly, it increases their chances of stroke and heart attack; if they don't exercise aerobically, it increases their chances by as much as 50% to be severely sick. It seemed that these threats weren't really having much of an impact on anyone.

I emphasized what we needed to do was point out the positive effects of making good health choices. I had been feeling and sounding very much on top of this subject until Lisa challenged me. "You try and scare us—Mom, my friends, me—into making healthier choices," she charged. She went on to say that everybody does it, that this is the way we have been trained to think in our society. Saying, "Stay away from this" and "Avoid that" because they are no good for you is a major method of getting people to do what is "good for them" according to the other person.

I went into ego shock. Other people use scare tactics, but I know better! I write the articles and do the workshops on wellness. No, surely not me!

Oh yes, it seemed, me too!

We really do have to remain alert if we are to stay positive in this negatively driven world. Many wellness promoters and programs base their strategies on the "big stick" approach, use lots of threats and fears and hope this will drive people to make better decisions. The problem is it doesn't work and, in fact, may put people at risk. What I learned that morning from my daughter was that:

- I need to ask for more feedback from others so I can spot my incongruities, and
- staying positive and being consistent requires a great deal of conscious attention and diligence.

If the fear method doesn't really work, why do we keep doing it? My flippant response is, "Just because it doesn't work has never stopped us before, right?" We keep trying to fit round pegs in square holes all the time.

So, let me approach this question in a different way. What is there about the negative approach that we find appealing, even if it doesn't work?

Firstly, let me state that scare tactics are instant attention grabbers, make great headlines, and spice up speeches and articles to impress upon listeners and readers the seriousness of their decisions. But as time passes and few changes are made, the effect is lost.

Secondly, some folks get excited instead of scared and push them self to the edge of that fear, leaving their health at risk. I am referring to people who are proud of the fact they smoke two-and-a-half packs of cigarettes a day and are still alive, or have never purposely exercised, or never buckled up in their car. They are proud of living on the edge.

Thirdly, people might give up hope if the fear campaign works too well. I remember reading some findings of the Cancer Society. They had done such a good job of reporting in the media as to what causes cancer that the public began to believe everything caused cancer and lost hope that they could really do anything to prevent it. They adopted a "what's the use" attitude, felt powerless to control their lives, and consequently stopped healthy practices, opting to rely on fate to determine their "wellness."

What I do believe—but obviously don't always practice—is that the promotion of wellness and a positive lifestyle is best served from the "half full cup" approach. Many more successes and permanent lifestyle changes will be influenced and achieved with the use of positive messages instead of these punishing negative ones.

What are some of the very simple approaches that help with the transition away from scaring people into action? An example is "Do this or die!" which should be replaced with messages that nurture and support, such as, "You'll feel so much better if you…!"

Try this exercise:

- Walk around your office, home or community and catch people doing something right
- Make a checklist of all the good stuff you do and are a part of each day in your worksite
- Train your eyes to see the strength in actions and spot natural abilities
- Perceive the beauty, serenity and health of your community and
- Look at your total life and list all the things that you already do and that you want to keep doing, consistent with your commitment to wellness.

If you are in some way responsible for the well-being of others or are merely promoting your own wellness, it is important to remember that the positive, half full approach is more effective and much more likely to produce long-term results than the scare method. People are more open to change and will do so if convinced there is a positive approach with a perceived payoff in it for them.

Thanks, Lisa!

The rule concerning exercise is simple. Miss one or two days, no problem, no chastising yourself, no guilt. However, if a third day is missed, it is my belief that a new behavior is starting, one that you do not want. So, the rule is simply two days okay, but never miss the third day.

DECLARING VS. FEAR OF FAILURE

The essence of a discussion with a client was, "Why do I procrastinate, end up with 20 things on my mind that I need to do, and then forget the most important of them?"

At first, I thought our discussion was going to be about prioritizing time and resources, but somewhere in the middle I realized we were talking about an irrational belief. Check this leap: The longer you leave things and then pull them together under extreme pressure, the more you look like a great magician/guru.

I realized that for many people, this pattern is really about a fear of failing. If I don't start a project until well into the time line, or if I'm late at a meeting and don't get all the details but still manage to pull the project off, I look real good. If I don't pull it off, if I fail, I don't look too bad because, well, I started late. This pattern is about having an excuse when or if I fail. It is about the fear of failure.

To fight the fear of failing, openly **declare** your wants, goals and objectives. Declaring requires you to be "in" or involved from the outset of the project. To state openly what you want, to put your hat in the ring, so to speak, is to not be controlled by a fear of failing. Not declaring your wants is very hard on your self-esteem, and although scary, declaring most often leads to a vastly increased self-esteem. Please change the following statement:

> *"We are not supposed to get what we want, rather we are supposed to do what we should!"*

LIFESTYLE IS THE GOAL...
HEALTH IS THE MEANS

In the process of living, we set many objectives and goals for ourselves. One of the most important of these is to be healthy. However, despite the fact that health is extremely important, it should not be the focus of our life. Health flows from our choices on how we live our life, our lifestyle.

To achieve balance in our lives, we must pay heed to the **holistic dimensions**: emotional, intellectual, work, spiritual, physical, and social (see *Appendix A*, page 138). It is to our advantage to consciously figure out a way of living so these dimensions are balanced. We need:

- To exercise, to eat properly, to get required sleep
- To have challenging and worthwhile work and endeavor in our lives
- To be intellectually stimulated through conversation, literature, theatre and study
- To have people with whom we can share our thoughts and feelings, who raise our spirits, and who give us positive strokes for "being" as well as "doing"
- To take time to appreciate beauty…sunsets, art, literature, flowers in the kitchen
- To help others

Health is not the primary focus in our lives, but a means to achieve what we want out of life.

A quality lifestyle is the goal.
Health is the means.

PURPOSE

Ever since my doctoral days at the University of Alberta, I have been impressed with the work of Dr. Victor Frankl. His writings are based on his experience in the Nazi work camps at Auschwitz. Frankl concluded that the difference between those who survived the camp experience and those who didn't—apart from those actually killed in the camps—was an attitude called "purpose in life." People who gave meaning to their lives survived; those who had no vision or purpose died. In essence, purpose gives us a reason to live, a meaning that transcends the horror and/or mundaneness of daily living.

The Meaning of Life issue, whether it be Frankl's or Monty Python's, has always been a bit heavy for my liking. I don't believe I need to solve this great riddle to enable me to have a great life. However, it is clear to me that I felt the most in control of my life; the most focused, the most alive, and had the highest self-esteem when I was on a quest, when I had a definite purpose in mind.

It might have been starting university, courting my wife-to-be, raising children, going for a job I wanted, preparing myself for a marathon, performing in theatre and facing those infamous and challenging opening nights, or pursuing my doctorate—being focused and having a purpose certainly made me feel alive.

As I approached my 68th birthday, I decided that I no longer wanted any large, time-consuming single-focus purposes in life. What I wanted instead were a bunch, a flock or perhaps a gaggle of little purposes. Not one big purpose but a bunch of little ones to keep me busy, focused, and feeling worthwhile—and would give meaning to my life.

If we believe most things are relative, then my little purposes at age 68 are just as important as someone else's major goals at age 36. The important thing that I learned from Frankl is that there is great strength in individuals if they learn to focus, if they **create a meaningful goal** for themselves and then **purposefully set out to accomplish that goal**.

LOWER THE BAR AND RAISE YOUR SPIRITS

I have learned that people who have recent physical disabilities or disorders and who are depressed/anxious about not being able to live their lives as they once did, need to help themselves by accepting their present level of ability. Extremely easy to say, but…! However, they need to do the most that they can with what they have, be who they are now, and not try to be who they were in the past.

They need to help themselves by changing their perspective or attitude to one based not only on what they can do to make their lives better, but more importantly, what will enable them to discover positives in themselves.

What I would encourage is for them to experience a "little" success and not look for the cure. They must not allow themselves to be overwhelmed with depression because then they experience only negatives based on what they can't do.

They could choose to feel better about consistently showing up at the gym, even though they are not able to do the things there that they did in the past. Even though they can do only some, maybe just a few, of the things they used to do, that is a positive gain. Congratulations are in order for success, no matter how small the measure.

The goal is to feel good about consistently doing small, do-able activities and accepting the small successes. The focus should then be on what they can do to motivate themselves to do even more.

Where health has been altered, people need to accept their new reality, that their **bar has been lowered**. Learn to be proud about what you can achieve instead of being depressed about what can no longer be done. Once again, easy to say, but…

Selye states that spice (variety)
is a prerequisite for a healthy life.

Feeling excitement about present positive accomplishments is vastly
superior to feeling negative about what one can no longer do.

MOVE YOUR FEET

I am not a country music fan; jazz is more my thing. However, "The Dance" by Garth Brooks has tremendous meaning for me. When my time comes to make "a move"—as my Trinidadian friends say—and to find out what it is really like on the other side of life, I don't want any regrets about how this life went. As Garth says, "I'll take my chances, make my mistakes, but I do not want to miss the **dance** in this life."

It was this song that influenced a session I recently had with a client. She was stuck, fearful of upcoming changes in her life, and overwhelmed by the infinite number of possibilities for her life. I wanted her to understand that change can be handled more easily if broken down into small pieces and dealt with one piece at a time. What came out of my mouth, a la Garth Brooks, was, "Just move your feet until it becomes a new dance." We laughed, and she understood what she needed to do—small and doable steps.

There is something to that dance analogy that gives us hope and the courage to confront life. When things are broken down into small enough components in which we believe we can succeed, then our lives feel more under control and we can start to make changes.

So, when you are feeling overwhelmed by circumstances in your life, remember to reframe the challenge and just move your feet in little steps until it becomes an exciting new dance.

*Take care of your feet first
so that you can help take care of others later in the dance.*

DEFLECTION THEORY

Deflect...don't absorb.

I believe it is necessary to learn how to effectively deal with aggressive people, because they are in our lives. It is important to learn how to **deflect their cannon balls**.

Often, we stand in front of the aggressor's verbal blast like a circus strongman who stops steel balls shot from a cannon with his stomach. Similarly, we must learn how to deflect the aggressor's verbal blast past us, instead of internalizing the negative energy.

Deflect negative energy and ideas and don't absorb them. Listen to a person's thoughts, feelings, values and beliefs, but don't accept them as "the" truth, only "their" truth. Take what makes sense but don't accept it all. Each of us has our own perception of "truth."

A **deflection** might sound like this: "Thank you for sharing your thoughts, values, feelings and beliefs with me. I appreciate what you say; however, it is not how I see it."

We need to take a page out of a Judo handbook if we want to learn how to deflect another person's energy, how to step aside and let the strength of their aggression—verbal or physical—pass us. These individuals certainly have power and believe they are right, but we don't have to stand still and be their target, absorb their negative energy, agree with what they perceive as truth. We can deflect, not fight, and then introduce our own truth. The real truth is that both truths are valid.

KILLER WORDS

In our vocabulary, there are words we use daily that make us sick, that are, in fact, killing us. I'll give you examples of killer words and then you can use the space provided to identify your own. When you've identified three to five killer words, write to me, share your words, and tell me how you plan to make yourself healthier.

Should is a killer word. Whenever the word comes to mind, I look over my shoulder and look for whoever said it. It's in my head but it's not me saying it. Perhaps I'm not the only one who needs to stop "should-ing" on them self?

Professional is a killer word. My definition of this is a person with no boundaries. Imagine believing that because you are a professional, you should continue until all the work is done with no or few restrictions. I've done this in the past and I see a great many professionals who choose to have few boundaries when it comes to work. There are far too many who adhere to my definition of "professional." I believe that many who hold this belief will eventually become ill and will choose, or be forced, to leave their profession.

Can I help? Killer phrase! It leaves me open to the "rescuer" in me. And that gets me into activities and responsibilities I don't really want. Perhaps the phrase I could better chose to use is, "Who else could you get to help you if I wasn't available?" or "What have you done in the past that's worked and didn't include me?" or, the big one, "If I died, how would you handle this issue?

Perhaps you have a list of favorite killer words or phrases and what they mean to you. Please, let me know.

1. _____
2. _____
3. _____
4. _____
5. _____

Contact me!: danrosin@mymts.net

TAKE CARE OF SELF FIRST

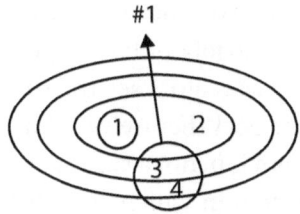

In an ideal world, Number (1) in the above diagram would be you and you would be number one when it comes to how you spend your time, how you spend your energy, how you **take care of self**. Number (2) would be your significant other, spouse, partner, and the person to whom you are most committed to outside of yourself. Number (3) would be children or other family members, and Number (4) would be your job.

In reality, what I see in my clients and previously in myself is there is no (1), (2) barely exists, and (3) and (4) hog most of the time and energy and end up becoming priority one.

It can be said that the children of educators are very well taken care of, getting more than their share of a parent's time and energy. They are encouraged to take up dancing, baseball, singing, music and soccer. Who takes them to all these activities? Their parents, and that is usually after they finish their incredibly stressful and energy-demanding teaching job. Once again, educators are prime **time** and **energy** givers. So, it is the kids at home (3) and the job (4) that get the majority of an educator's best time and energy.

Prevalent among educators today is an unchecked slide to burnout, poor health, and strained relationship issues. I don't see it changing until individuals understand that they have to:

- take care of themselves, and
- take care of their primary relationship.

The permission to take care of oneself first comes from understanding the words of Hans Selye, and I paraphrase: the reason you take good care of yourself, eat properly, exercise, network, is so that you will have more to give to others. Until educators learn how to do that, the avalanche of poor health will continue.

Perhaps giving yourself permission to take care of you and your partner without feeling guilty and without always putting kids and job first, is the starting point for improving your health. Even without kids, many funnel their best time and energy into jobs or taking care of aging family members, friends and/or pets. Many educators see their jobs as the most important thing in their lives, and neglect themselves and significant others.

Remember **teaching is a job, not a calling**. I realize that much resultant ill health is due to the system in which educators work. Many invitations to become ill stem from a system that cares more about people on the outside than those on the inside. There are people who do well at battling—our union reps—the system's inequalities, unfair treatment, and negative expedient decisions on our behalf. They have become adept and have an interest in applying their political skills. While they are doing that, it allows the educator in the schools to do their job. However educators need to stop blaming the system as the total cause of ill health and burnout and must discover or revert to personal regimes that put them into the best shape—physically, psychologically, spiritually—that they have ever been.

Lift weights instead of pointing fingers. Choose to spend time doing enjoyable activities with your special people. Satisfy your own needs (not just your kids') rather than be a couch potato, always complaining that "things are not what they used to be." Running a mile will not improve the people skills of a poor administrator with whom you deal, but it certainly will enable the runner to deal more effectively with that administrator. As the Nike ad says, "Just Do It!" To that I add, "Just Do It Consistently." Make sure it's for yourself, to your liking, with people who make you laugh.

Take care of your self first—then take care of others!

*I can't control all the curve balls thrown at me in my life,
but I can be in charge of how I deal with them.*

STAND AND DELIVER

I rented a movie, hoping to be entertained, but also because I felt a bit "homesick" for the classroom and teaching. I had been out of the classroom about eight years, so I chose a movie with an educational theme. The movie was called "Stand and Deliver" and it turned out to be simultaneously a most entertaining and disturbing film.

If memory serves me correctly, it is about a teacher in Los Angeles who assists a class of students to become the first group from their school to pass their college entrance tests (calculus had always been their downfall). The teacher gave up evenings, weekends and summer holidays to help students understand their mathematics. I remember that his health was affected, and his relationship with his wife and family were strained, but apparently the trade-off was that his students did give him a plaque for his efforts. My first thought was that he was a hero, just like the director of the film intended me to think. However, as more and more of the rescuing/martyr-type behavior continued, I wanted to throw up.

The very next day, as coincidence would have it, a teacher I had been counselling who had issues dealing with a lack of self-care, stated in her session that her principal had been showing a film for the past two noon hours to teachers. The intention in showing the film was that the staff would become more like the character in the film. My client was feeling extremely uncomfortable with this. The film, coincidentally, was "Stand and Deliver." We discussed our mutual feelings about the film and when I said I wanted to throw up, a big smile crossed her face.

"You know, until you said that, I was feeling so guilty because all I could think of was if one more person expected me to be more than I can humanly be, I will throw up all over them." We laughed almost hysterically, but we both knew the problem that this film triggered wasn't about the system wanting teachers to do more. No, the real problem was about the caregiver who cared so much and was so driven that he was willing to give up his life, his marriage and his family for the job. We make heroes out of people like this every day in our society!

Let's hope that the next generation of caregivers might be content doing a good job, a realistic job, and then stop at the end of the day, that they learn to **kiss the bricks goodbye** and go home to a **Real Life** with their family and friends. Perhaps **balance** is a better goal than heroism.

20% of the students get 80% of your time and energy. Work with the students who want to learn, and don't be angry with those who don't. Continue to motivate and encourage your students, but stop giving so much time and energy to those who aren't happy and productive in your class. The harder you work, the more they will let you.

If you keep doing what you're doing, you'll keep getting what you're getting.

PROFESSIONAL

My definition of a "professional" is a person who has few boundaries when it comes to their work. Some teachers have fallen victim to **Romantic Professional Image Syndrome** (RPIS), a view that is encouraged by the media, the entertainment culture, their School Division, and driven by the individual's own obsessive belief in hard work—all the time.

Most educators, as well as other professionals, start their careers as caring, committed and idealistic people. However, after about seven or eight years of meeting the system's needs and only occasionally their own, educators begin to burn out. At least that was my jaded observation as a therapist working in an educator EAP. What's your experience with burnout?

Educators' thoughts turn to wondering what life would be like if they did something else for a living. They begin to make plans, at least in their heads, to leave their chosen profession. Have you ever done that?

We need a strong dose of realism as to what is possible and what we can accomplish. We must understand that to be helpful to others, we must first help ourselves. Because we are professionals does not mean we have to sacrifice ourselves for the job. Being a professional could mean finding the balance between doing a good job and having a good life.

I want to live and teach, not die because I teach!

EDUCATORS OUGHT TO BUY SEASON TICKETS TO EVERYTHING

At one of my workshops for educators on "Taking Care of Yourself," I learned that more preparation was not the most important pastime that I wanted in the teachers who taught my children.

A very burned-out teacher who had been challenging me all day on my sense of humor and stories with a point—at least I thought they had a good point—finally had enough of me when I stated rather flippantly that I believe educators, as well as most caregivers, should buy **season tickets** to everything. I suggested that if they go to an activity, they have at least created the potential for having fun, since getting them out and away from busy work schedules is the real problem. I added that educators who buy season tickets will go—no matter what—because they are cheap, um, I mean frugal and will want to attend so they won't be seen—by themselves or anyone else—as wasting their money.

Having taught in schools for 20 years, I thought I could poke fun at my self and others in the profession. However, this teacher took umbrage and blurted out, "If your child were in my class, you would be the first to complain about me not being well prepared and spending my evenings enjoying myself instead of working at lesson preparation."

Interestingly enough, my child was in this teacher's class and it was clear by his response that he was burned-out and obviously missing a great many such details. So, I responded to his claim about the need to be perfectly prepared: "For the teachers of my children, I really would prefer you to be moderately prepared in your class lessons. However, I insist you be an exciting teacher, and so I ask just how can a person be an exciting teacher if they are not excited about their own life?"

In my practice, I see a great many well-prepared educators who, in fact, are killing themselves to keep their standards up. I believe that educators work themselves into a workaholic lifestyle and eventually lose the ability to be excited about their own lives. It shows in their health and in their classroom attitude.

You need to get out to more fun activities, create a little more variety and spice in your life. See change as a welcome thing, something different that will contribute to the excitement of your own life. Then you will have the ability to pass that excitement on to your students and others in your life.

Your job (teaching) is to give strokes (units of recognition), not get strokes (at the workplace). Your needs get met in your "Real Life." So, make sure you have one!

One of the biggest stressors in Education today is the lack of cooperation and concern between educators.

Judge your success in life by the degree you enjoy good health, happiness, and quality of life.

IF YOU CAN'T STAND THE HEAT, GET OUT OF THE KITCHEN

People often get angry with me when I refer to teaching as a "job," not a "calling." At a recent workshop, an angry individual stood up and told me that she felt so deeply about being a teacher that she did see it as a "calling."

At these times, I wish the system—the Board, the superintendents, the Principal, the taxpayers—would appreciate, defend, cherish and look after those people who dedicate their lives to the "calling." However, instead of being defended, they are often abused. Educators are expendable because, in the past, there have been more teachers than jobs. Somebody's waiting in the wings when one falls, and they take up the "calling" until they fall. I realize I am extremely jaded as I view this tragedy, but I personally know hundreds of teachers who have succumbed to stress and burnout and physical-related illnesses.

I feel I must warn those who are all too willing to sacrifice themselves that it might be "nice" if teaching was thought of as a "calling," that teachers would be revered, loved and respected instead of treated as expendable and replaceable. I quote a superintendent: *If you can't stand the heat, get out of the kitchen*. However, the world isn't "nice" and teachers aren't particularly revered, loved and respected, no matter how much they do!

Our leaders—Board, superintendents, governments—and the people we serve directly—students and parents—need to realize that we are human beings with needs that include being treated with respect. We need to be in a balanced partnership to find solutions to the extreme difficulties that we face in Education today. Until that shift in respect and power occurs, we had best figure out how to do this job of teaching with a realistic approach to time and energy so that we can stay healthy. It is my feeling that "callings" need to be left for those in the service of God, and even then I wonder.

I am concerned for individuals who hide their head in the sand and say, "It will never happen to me" (burnout, stress, anxiety, depression, physical deterioration). They keep up their workaholic pace and critically judge colleagues who are finding a life outside of their job.

Much of the time, we are not very nice to colleagues who "do not do their share," meaning that we actually get angry and attack people who know how to have a life. Instead of seeing their choice to use their time and energy in a healthy way, we choose to glorify our driven behavior and stroke ourselves if we are the last to leave school, or when we go one-up when it comes to demonstrating the dedication and long hours invested in our jobs.

We need to start emphasizing a balanced approach to living. Working hard is good, but so is having a life! We need to stop judging and criticizing colleagues who take time to have a life, and instead we should be giving them awards (i.e., *Balanced Educator Award*, see *Appendix B*, page 140).

When advertising for new teachers, we might consider saying: "Teaching is a job, a very important job, but not worth giving up your life for. Overly dedicated, sacrificial and martyr-type inclined people need not apply. Only persons who understand and practice a balanced lifestyle need apply."

For some people, there is the necessity of making their jobs a "calling" because they don't know how, or are too frightened, or are just not willing to take responsibility for developing a real life. If they don't know how to have a life anyway, or have forgotten how, they might just as well work long and hard and be rewarded by the system.

Been there, done that. No thanks!

Teaching school is not a "glorified" mission.
It is a job! It is work!

BADMINTON ON THE ED SULLIVAN SHOW (JUST LIKE TEACHING)

You teach, they learn!

One rare day, I was sitting in my office with my feet up on my desk—after an incredibly busy and productive day, of course—when some pictures started floating through my mind. They were images from the old television program,"The Ed Sullivan Show." I remembered the badminton player who played badminton by himself. Served, ran to the other side of the net, returned behind the back, over the neck, through the legs—very entertaining.

The significance of these memories was at first in question, but then it became clear. I realized that teaching had become much like that badminton performance, where you served—teachers taught a lesson— and then you ran to the other side of the net—you took responsibility for students learning. It's true that the system—administration, parents and children—expects you to take responsibility for the student's learning, but for Pete's sake, don't buy into something so impossible as taking responsibility for somebody else's learning. We should only take responsibility for our **teaching**.

This is one of the major reasons for the **burning out** of educators. You're playing mostly by yourself, doing the serving—teaching—and returning—learning—and the students are becoming less and less responsible participants in the process.

Near the end of my Ed Sullivan fantasy, the image had developed into a teacher running back and forth hitting the bird, running to the other side returning the bird—teaching, then taking responsibility for learning, so that after a while the students just sat down at the net and watched the teacher killing himself. The clincher is this: the students who are sitting at the net, watching the teacher dash madly and desperately back and forth, get whiplash and sue the teacher—because the teacher is running too hard. Fantasy? Hmm!

You need to understand, and help others to understand, that you can only teach. Teaching is your job and your students need to take responsibility for their own learning. I suppose about now we could deviate into a discussion on how good teachers can help motivate their students to want to take responsibility for their own learning. This discussion is definitely warranted, but not in this context.

To a teacher moving into a new program:

- *the less you create—take over—and the more you assist and encourage others—mainly students—to create, the better job you will be doing; and*
- *if you are going to be successful with kids, they had better own the program—not you. You are the facilitator and not the owner of the program.*

DISCIPLINE AND THE THREE CS

It is my belief that you cannot successfully discipline a student if you don't have a relationship with that student. You need to have them realize their behavior, take ownership for it, and consider making a different choice next time.

Successful discipline begins with my sharing with students and having them think about their behavior. I do not think this is possible unless they are open to hearing me. That openness comes from a relationship, and from their believing that I have their best interests at heart. I may be upset and angry at their behavior, but I still like them. If I don't like the student, they will perceive that and, in most cases, disciplining them will not be successful. I need to demonstrate **caring**, **courtesy** and **concern**, and so does the student.

The ability to discipline a student starts long before the event that requires the discipline. Rarely will today's students be influenced by a person's position, such as a teacher. They will heed only those they trust.

Successful discipline is the result of a trusting relationship.

DISPENSER OF POSITIVE REMINDERS

I am sure educators are often uncertain as to what their role really is. Are they teachers, counsellors, disciplinarians, coaches, nurses, parent designates, or all of the above?

I would add to that list an additional role that is certainly happening but apparently has not been given a name. I call this role the **dispenser of positive reminders**.

It is used by educators who do not wish to punish students into changing their behavior but rather are interested in positively reminding students of their commitment to change. More specifically, these educators continually remind students about how they might want to change their lives.

People will change if the threat of punishment is severe enough. The problem with punishment is that it stops working the moment the threat is removed. Fear-motivated change is only temporary.

Being positive, recognizing the positive qualities in people, and encouraging people by exhibiting positive behavior toward them will allow these same people to feel good about themselves and to feel safe. Then, the changes they make are more apt to be permanent.

People want to do and be their best and are willing to commit to change, but only when they feel **safe** and **trusting**. Being human, they need to be **positively reminded** of their commitment to change when they are off track, and **positively rewarded** when they are on track.

NOBODY GETS IN MY WAY OF TEACHING

Things weren't going well in the classroom. Kids were being disruptive and not settling down. The teacher had just about given up any hope of finding a way to handle them and their unsympathetic parents. Nothing seemed to be working. And although what came out of my mouth was meant to be helpful, it was neither good counselling nor an accepted therapeutic intervention.

It had been 15 years since I was in charge of a classroom and I was on shaky ground. I was not sure it was appropriate but, nonetheless, blurted out the following directive:

"I am a teacher. I get paid to teach and nobody, and I mean nobody, will be allowed to prevent me from doing that. I will not allow a student to continually disrupt my class and prevent other students from learning." It seemed to strike a meaningful chord with the teacher.

This approach of dealing with students who continue to disrupt class, despite many invitations to conform to normal classroom behavior, needs to be direct and focused on the fact that they are disrupting the learning of the other students. However, we need both the administration and the parents on our side when we confront.

Parents don't really care if the teacher is upset or their kid's behavior is really stressful and wearing the teacher down. It is not considered legitimate by either the administration or parents if the reason the child was expelled from the classroom was because their behavior was somehow disturbing the teacher. However, if we explain that the child was preventing other students from learning, this may receive more understanding.

"I don't get mad at students who cut up in my class. I invite them to change their behavior at least twice before asking them to leave the class. I explain to them and their parents that I won't allow anyone to prevent me from doing my job, which is teaching students who have chosen not to disrupt the class and intend to learn. I don't get mad at disruptive students, I simply invite them to change their disruptive behavior or ask them to leave for that period or day. Tomorrow is another day and we start over, expecting the best."

If we let students, parents and administrators know that we will not put up with disruptive students because they prevent other students from learning; we may receive more cooperation than if they think we are just chucking kids out of our classes because they bother us. In the climate we find ourselves teaching today, we had better find a stronger position than "that student was disruptive" before we can have them removed from class. Despite how valid I believe this approach is I know it will be challenged vigorously in some communities and schools.

Don't get mad—just do your job and focus on those who most want to learn.

How do you make a "not" happen—as in "That is not what I want you to do"? You can't! So, learn to state what you do want or will do, and not what you don't want or won't do.

PHILOSOPHICAL DILEMMA

Consider:

"Do I not have a life because I work so hard?"
　　or
"Do I work so hard because I do not know how to have a life?"
Either way, perhaps it is time to consider the following:

APPENDICES

Appendix A: Six Dimensions of Wellness

Appendix B: Balanced Educator Award

Appendix C: Glossary

APPENDIX A

SIX DIMENSIONS OF WELLNESS

EMOTIONAL

The emotional dimension emphasizes an awareness and acceptance of one's feelings. Emotional wellness includes the degree to which one feels positive and enthusiastic about oneself and life. It includes the capacity to manage one's feelings and related behaviors, including the realistic assessment of one's limitations, development of autonomy, and ability to cope effectively with stress. The emotionally well person maintains satisfying relationships with others.

INTELLECTUAL

The intellectual dimension encourages creative and stimulating mental activities. An intellectually well person uses the resources available to expand one's knowledge in improved skills, along with expanding potential for sharing with others. An intellectually well person uses the intellectual and cultural activities in and beyond the classroom, combined with the human and learning resources available within the university and the larger community.

WORK

The occupational dimension is involved in preparing for work in which one will gain personal satisfaction and find enrichment in one's life through work. Occupational development is directly related to one's attitude about one's work.

SPIRITUAL

The spiritual dimension involves seeking meaning and purpose in human existence. It includes the development of a deep appreciation for the depth and expanse of life and natural forces that exist in the universe.

PHYSICAL

The physical dimension encourages cardiovascular flexibility and strength as well as regular physical activity. Physical development encourages knowledge about food and nutrition and discourages the use of tobacco, drugs, and excessive alcohol consumption. It encourages involvement in activities that contribute to high-level wellness, including medical self-care and appropriate use of the medical system.

SOCIAL

The social dimension encourages contributing to one's human and physical environment for the common welfare of one's community. It emphasizes the interdependence with others and nature. It includes the pursuit of harmony in one's family.

Bill Hetler
National Wellness Association

APPENDIX B

BALANCED EDUCATOR AWARD (BEA)

I believe people should be rewarded for their balanced approaches and healthy attitudes toward their work. Here is a sample awards program I developed for teachers.

Would you be interested in beginning such a program in your school?

Award the teacher who best exemplifies balance between professionalism and having a "real life."

The purpose of such an award is to emphasize/highlight the importance of doing a good job (being professional) with having a balanced variety of fun and relaxing activities.

Colleagues nominate each other along with Administration.

As well as having the teacher's name on a certificate or plaque, the teacher receives a (nominal amount) gift voucher for a wellness activity (golf, gym) or sports equipment shop (toward walking shoes or some sports equipment).

Your local Teachers Association would supply certificates and promote the award.

Dan Rosin
Planned Action for Wellness

APPENDIX C

GLOSSARY

(Symbols, Words, Terms, Phrases)

(A)	Adult Ego State (Transactional Analysis Model)—gathers and processes information, little feeling, computer-like, asks questions
BEA	Balanced Educator Award, to be given each month to an educator whose lifestyle exemplifies high professional standards and a balanced lifestyle (see Appendix B)
burnout	the person is no longer able to perform even normal, everyday functions. The person has no drive, no desire, no energy. Stressed out, overwhelmed, circuits are overloaded—words used to describe the person's feelings
buffer Time	time used to relax and have fun in between work/projects
C	congruent, what we are thinking and feeling is what comes out our mouths
(C)	Child Ego State (Transactional Analysis Model)—intuition, feelings, sense of humor, spontaneous, creative, fun-loving
computer	brain
COs	Conscientious Objectors, persons who refused to fight during WWII

"danger" chemicals	the body produces chemicals to assist the body to deal with the danger
desired outcome	the outcome that is needed for one to feel successful and in control
"differences are strengths"	the individual differences people bring to a relationship should be viewed as a strength for that relationship. Differences provide more options and the result is a stronger "whole"
"do life"	living life to the fullest
Drama Triangle	a dysfunctional way of communicating using the roles of Rescuer, Victim, Persecutor (Tabi Kehler)
dysfunctional family	one that relates in unhealthy ways family of origin the family into which you were born
Fight or Flight Syndrome	the ability of the body to rally the chemicals it needs to fight or flee when threatened
gap	the natural space between two independent people. It's good they are different, but the relationship needs to be worked on so that the gap does not get too wide and they drift apart
health computer chip	messages on our brain in reference to health and well-being
"…here and now"	the present moment
holistic	principles of health that include the following dimensions: emotional, intellectual, work, spiritual, physical, social
hypnotic voice	quiet, calm, even paced, plants positive ideas
"It"	God, Buddha, Mohammed, Confucius—the Center of the Universe, "It." A human can never be "It"
"kiss the bricks goodbye"	leaving work at work *(Donald Meichenbaum)*

learned helplessness	one is taught (generally in family of origin) not to trust themselves to make good decisions, and so come to depend on others
Life Force Energy *(Selye)*	a finite source of energy the body possesses that we can use. We need a balanced lifestyle so that we don't exhaust the life force energy resource
lower the bar	lower one's expectations
monkeys	problems or issues
nurtured	loved and cared for
other language	the choice of words that indicates the person is committed to doing for others (and not self)
P + P = P	patience + pace = protection
payoff	the outcome, the motivating factor for the behavior in the first place
<P>	persecutor (Drama Triangle)
pleaser/placator	one who has been taught that the way to "make it" in the world is to be nice and helpful (to others, not self)
pot	the imaginary contouring in each human being where strokes are collected *(Virginia Satir)*
principles	what one thinks, feels, values, and believes
Pu + Pu	pushing and punishing
quality of life	people/activities that we deem to be fun and enjoyable, thus giving our lives a quality
Real Life	the most important part of our life (as opposed to work life)—time for self, partner, family, and friends
rehearsing	preparing a response instead of listening to the speaker
<R>	rescuer (Drama Triangle)

<R+>	rescuers rescue other people to get their own needs met
reverse mirror	you do the opposite to what the person in front of you is doing (speed up—slow down, loud—quiet)
RPIS	Romantic Professional Image Syndrome. Educators and the media idealize overworking
self-actualization	to be all you can be *(Maslow)*
self language	the choice of words that indicates the person is committed to health and self-care (not at the exclusion of others)
Six Dimensions of Wellness	(see Appendix A)
slurp out the color	suck out the excitement and many experiences life has to offer. Go for the gusto
Solution Focused	a school of therapy that focuses on solving people's problems, that looks at changing behavior in the present
spice	variety *(Selye)*
stroke	a unit of recognition
third family	creating new ways of interacting as a couple, instead of relying on behaviors learned from family of origin
T F V B	thoughts, feelings, values, beliefs
time out	a decision to walk away and cool off. Get a new perspective and then work to resolve the issue
three Cs	caring, courtesy, concern
type A	a person with a driven, hard-working personality. One whose focus is on work and accomplishment
<V>	victim (Drama Triangle)
WWII	World War II

| "Your behavior is understandable, but no longer appropriate" | knowing the person's early history and family of origin, their present behavior might be understandable. However, they are now older, they have personal power and the ability to make rational decisions, and their present behavior is no longer appropriate |

Also by Dan Rosin:

Communication and Relationships is a book composed of concepts derived from composites of many different sessions with many different clients. Concepts are insights into the how, where, and why of human behaviour and this is how we learn. It is my intent by sharing these concepts that the reader will have a better understanding of the process of good communication and other insights that work to improve their relationships and life.

The book is written for people who seek an understanding of the problems they face in their everyday lives. It is for anyone living in challenging relationships with feelings of distress, guilt, or anger, or who may be struggling to make a decision about that same relationship. They learn to appreciate they are not alone, and that others have similar issues and that they have found a way to proceed. By reading these concepts they can learn how to better deal with their own issues.

In the book I share **112 different concepts** (learning opportunities) ranging from 1-3 pages in length. Some of the topics other than relation-ships and communication include: stress, anger, grief, strokes, guilt, ego, self-esteem, change, affairs, sex and power, abandonment, friendship and more.

Communication & Relationships can be purchased on-line at www.theewingspublishing.com, Google, Amazon, Barnes & Noble.

www.ingramcontent.com/pod-product-compliance
Lightning Source LLC
LaVergne TN
LVHW041950070526
838199LV00051BA/2975